HYPNOTISM LEXICON BY LOIS PRINZ

The Heart of Hypnosis
and
Deep Healing Workbook

A Primer of Hypnotic Induction and Emergence
SCRIPTS FOR THE HYPNOTIST

as spoken by
Emmett Miller, MD

annotated by
Lois Prinz, CH

DISCLAIMER

These products are not presented as a complete training in hypnosis or psychology, but as valuable adjuncts for use by practitioners who are legally qualified to employ them and for nonprofessionals who wish a deeper understanding of the functioning of the human mind-body system. They are not substitutes for required medical or psychological treatment.

Copyright © 2010 Miller / Prinz
All Rights Reserved.

ISBN: 1558410139
ISBN-13 9781558410138

"By choosing certain kinds of thoughts and images, a person is able to control how they see the world, what they are aware of (and not aware of), and how they think about or process their perceptions."

When I first discovered the science of hypnosis back in 1969, I found it changed my medical practice, and gradually my whole life, in very significant ways. As I became more aware of the nature of tools of hypnosis, I began to discover that they were being employed, intentionally and unintentionally, in many aspects of our lives. To help the healthcare profession and the general population learn about these extraordinarily effective tools, I began to refer to them in my classes and publications using more approachable words as Guided Imagery, Deep Relaxation or Selective Awareness. Building on the metaphorical relationship between the computer and the human mind, I also refer to hypnosis as Software for the Mind.

Learning the basic tools of hypnosis can be of great value, even if you are not a health care professional, coach, yoga teacher, or trainer. The principles you will acquire throughout this training will find great application in many areas of your life – in fact, in all those interactions and relationships with others where you want to be truly respectful of them assisting them to be happier, to enjoy their relationship to you and grow from the experience. You will understand how to interact with people so as to maximize creativity and productivity through building rapport, respect and confidence. You will learn the language of suggestion and how to get the most out of your relationships that express themselves more fully in your presence.

The perspective you receive will also help you to better understand what people are really trying to communicate to you. This will enable you to form a more accurate and useful assessment (diagnosis); the more correct your assessment, the more effective the therapy you will design.

Further, you will discover these tools will provide you with effective ways of responding so as to support high-level wellness, healing and peak performance in those you serve and those you love.

Learning the basics of hypnosis, how its tools and techniques affect people's beliefs and behaviors, can enable you to assist others to think and act more wisely. These are only a few of the ways you will find this training can affect your life.

What is Hypnosis?

The most succinct definition I know of hypnosis is "suggestion during focused attention." In modern hypnotherapy, the state of focused attention we use is generally a state of deep relaxation – something very akin to a state of deep meditation or prayer. It is to a person in this highly receptive, highly responsive state of mind that we offer suggestions, and invite them to entertain those suggestions; to hold them in mind.

Hypnosis is not therapy, but a state of mind in which therapy can be performed to great advantage. Similarly, hypnosis is not coaching, counseling or teaching, but a medium that can enhance and empower. The tools of hypnosis allow us to construct a series of images that become the vehicle through which healing (making whole) concepts are delivered to the psyche, mind, emotions and body. Specific hypnotic states are employed to increase the penetration and power of these images and the deeper truth they symbolize.

I prefer the following perspective on therapeutic hypnosis:

> There is no one "hypnotic state": there are many states of consciousness that we experience and / or and that we may be guided into.
>
> We hold a collection of tools and skills that enables us to move into and out of various states of consciousness, and guide awareness so as to enhance or diminish certain patterns of thinking, feeling, behaving, believing and relating to others and the environment.
>
> Certain states of consciousness have particular clinical usefulness. I refer to these as Therapeutic States of Hypnosis. In these states, the subject is receptive, relaxed, trusting, emotionally responsive and focused.

In a sense, every state of consciousness, including the stupor of denial most people walk around in, can be thought of as a different "trance" state. Our clients may be thought of as coming to us in a trance state that is maladaptive – they come to us having been hypnotized into believing limiting images of them-selves and their potential. Our job then is to dehypnotize them by making the suggestion tools of hypnosis available so they can be used to enhance health and healing. Perhaps the only non trance state is total enlightenment.

The phenomenon of hypnosis leads to the discovery of an incredibly powerful tool for directing the perceptions and behaviors of one and others.

Hypnotic Suggestion and Tools of the Trade

The suggestions we use are auditory, visual, kinesthetic stimulation – by spoken word or music; photos, videos, digital images; or emotive by nature. Our therapeutic goal is to create a series of images that will have a healing, balancing, stimulating and empowering effect upon the behavior of the client mind. In other words, we induce relaxation and help people create mental images. Sometimes these image suggestions are direct, sometimes indirect.

Accordingly, the "suggestions" given in hypnosis are exactly that, *suggestions.* There is no demand, no judgment or criticism, no shaming, guilting, or manipulation. There is simply the offering of intelligent, wise options. When uttered to a person in a hypnotic state, suggestions prove powerful, even life changing because they are being heard within the very special context of a trusting relationship.

Clearly, all suggestion during focused concentration is not necessarily supportive of good health or productive for individual healing. A child with his or her attention raptly focused on a TV cartoon character that is selling them Sweet Tooth Sugar-Coated Corn Flakes and saying, "They're G-r-r-eat" provides an example of the manipulative use of hypnotic tools that are not necessarily in the best interest of the subject!

It is our belief that each person has a deep knowing concerning what they really want and need. For that reason, we employ the kinds of suggestion which help elicit from the subject what is truly needed, and which help to support healing images that arise from the subject. These are known as "permissive suggestions."

These differ from the kinds of suggestions that may be used by a political party, stage hypnotist or advertiser of a new car or cat food. After all, we are not trying to convince that patient/client to buy some particular product, join a particular organization, or believe in a certain religion or political party.

Perfect Practice Makes Perfect

People seem to see hypnosis as a kind of one-shot deal; you would see a hypnotist, be hypnotized, and if you were a "good subject," you would receive great benefit. If not, then you were labeled a "poor subject" and oh well.... On the other hand, if people could re-enter a hypnotic state and receive health-giving suggestions a number of times, many more could be helped.

I began to realize that multiple visits provided an opportunity for training (or re-training) of the mind to take place. Just as practicing your scales on the piano enables you to better play the music you want to play, re-entering the deeply relaxed state (self-hypnosis), and repeating the suggestions and affirmations constituted a mental training. However, back in those days, few people had any way to take home recorded experiences and repeatedly rehearse the suggestions.

Then came what, to me was one of the greatest inventions of all time – the cassette tape. I was thrilled! Now all one had to do was to purchase an inexpensive cassette player and play back recordings made in the office. This re-exposed the subject to not only the words, but also my voice speaking at the appropriate speed, pacing, rhythm, texture, tonality and music of my suggestions multiple times each day. The potential for healing, wellness and peak performance became multiplied with the onset of recorded sessions. Today my recordings of self-healing and mind-body healing are viral; healthcare providers and their patients and clients passed the word along that there was another way to approach illness and dysfunction.

Designing a Hypnotic Process: Creating Software for Your Mind

Software for the Mind reflects the similarity that an effective sequence of images for the mind is to the sequence of instructions given a computer by its programmer. These images comprise a set of instructions for how you want your nervous system (and the rest of your body) to see and interpret the world, and how you want to respond and act.

When an advertiser or political group designs an advertisement or a commercial, they design into it hypnotic language and suggestion that is intended to get you to buy their product, service or candidate. Their goal is pretty much 100% to make more money for themselves, not to make you happy. The sales team gets salary increases based on the revenue they generate, not upon how happy the customer is. In a sense, designing a hypnotic process is very much like writing a commercial or advertisement. The critical difference is that your goal is to sell health, excellence, happiness and success; the tools of thoughts and mental images enabling your system to behave in a manner that can create these outcomes most reliably in your life. The goal is to sell you on the belief that you possess, at a deep level, wisdom and intelligence. You have the power to truly know yourself and guide yourself towards serving your deepest values, expressing yourself, achieving success, happiness and Love. You are also selling a set of tools that will serve many purposes, and the ability to build faith in those tools so that they continue to become even more useful and powerful.

Right Relationship

The secret power of the therapeutic hypnosis process stems from the relationship the therapist creates with the subject, patient or client. After all, a therapist or coach is, first of all, a caring, wise, sensitive and nurturing friend. You intentionally establish a relationship that is designed to be respectful, appreciative, acknowledging, supportive and inspiring.

Your creating a special relationship has created a bond characterized by confidence, positive expectation and faith. Your practice taught you to look for and to see the deeper value of each person – an essential worth beyond any imperfections. You believe in them, and they believe in you.

There are three factors that fully determine each choice and each decision you make in life. Our ability to be clear about these three factors will have a profound influence on our success or failure, health or illness.

The first factor is your own internal image of yourself – what do you believe about yourself, are you valuable or worthless, good or bad, capable of loving or not? The second factor is what you believe about the world around you and the people in it – is this a safe place or a battlefield; are you surrounded by ugliness and hatred, or by beauty and love; is it a place where success and healing are possible? The third factor is the relationship you imagine exists between you and the world and the people in it.

Of particular importance is how you see the people you treat, counsel or coach. I have found it best to believe that each person we see has certain qualities that are unique and special to him or her. Some of these are gifts, skills and talents they can use; other qualities serve as impediments or liabilities. Our job is to assist them in identifying and nurturing the former, and in learning to overcome or transform the latter. We call this healing, personal growth and optimal or peak performance.

The relationship evoked by the kind of guidance, suggestions and images we use reflects a relationship of mutual respect, sense of connection, shared values and trust. By drawing upon the powerful forces that becomes available during such a relationship, we catalyze positive change and transformation.

We believe there is great power within each person, denied to them because they have never acquired the tools and skills that can give them access to this inner treasure. The primary objective is to promote this inner project to the person and market it to them, as if we are a P.R. agency for the client's soul or deeper self.

Our first job is to discover as much as possible about the person, how they communicate, how they perceive, what are their styles of learning (E.G., are they primarily auditory, visual or kinesthetic learners?). Next we need to carefully explore, question and discover what the person really wants. Their stated reason for coming may be a headache, or being able to sleep better – whereas, what it turns out they really need, on deeper exploration, is to let go of a resentment they have been holding onto.

It is best to see hypnosis as a co-creative process, a relationship of a special kind between you and client. Be flexible to alter your program and your interaction with clients as you explore you interaction / relationship as it emerges with them.

There are many ways we strive to help a person achieve a particular state of mind (such as deep relaxation) and to guide their mental images in such a way as to produce the most desirable outcome. Beyond the dictionary meaning of the words we use, there is also the tempo and rhythm of our sentence, the tone and timbre of our voice, the skillful use of pauses, - even the sincerity of the spoken word "good!" These can be appreciated and learned by listening to the original recording from which the transcription you are reading was made. By the way, these can be found for instant download or on CD at http://www.DrMiller.com.

It is our desire that you will learn the poetic phraseology is actually built upon sound scientific and therapeutic principles. As you learn, feel free to develop ways of using poetic structures, figures of speech and other artistic elements in a communication, as long as they are congruent with the principles and theory you have learned in this program.

Good Luck...And Enjoy

Please let yourself enjoy the learning process. From the beginning, you will find people quite grateful for how much comfort and peace you can give them, even with the most elementary of hypnotic experiences. As you enjoy feeling how good it feel to be an agent of positive change, your self-confidence will grow, and you will find that each new lesson brings more success and healing to your patients and clients.

A Note on How to Best Use This Book…

By now, you have probably already browsed through this book, read the Preface by Dr. Miller, and peeked at my Lexicon so you have some idea as to the format to this book.

More specifically, my explanation of Dr. Miller's carefully chosen words are in *italics* on the far right side of each page margin. I have right justified my comments in regards to Dr. Miller's poetic delivery in the hopes you will come to better understand and master the mechanics to the hypnotic process. This includes awareness of Pre-Talk, Induction, Deepening, Suggestion Management, Spiritual Growth and Emerging. (You can catch post-dialog on Deep Healing: Heart of Hypnosis DVD.)

The page across from the patter page is intentionally left blank so you may keep your own personal notes or create suggestions specifically for the client in front of you. This workbook is meant to be used, digested, processed and formed into your own voice and intentionality.

Notice how you can choose a different induction from the many Dr. Miller offers and combine it with an unlimited combination of deepening phrases to provide the spiritual resources (e.g. Inner Healer) the client will draw upon manifesting transformation and positive change. You also will quickly come to learn how skillfully Dr. Miller calls the Listener back to awareness and Emerging, as he provides us with some of the best modeling of contemporary hypnosis available.

Oh, one more thing, a Lexicon is a collection of words related to a similar concept, in this case, hypnosis. At the end of this manual, I have compiled a fairly comprehensive list of professional verbiage regarding the many aspects of hypnotherapy so you can feel free to use it as a more thorough explanation and clarification of my side notes. Also, check out Dr. Miller's definitions of Guided Energy, Deep Relaxation, Selective Awareness and Guided Imagery.

I am honored and humbled to have been asked to create this deserving companion to a fabulous Spiritual Hypnotism training. Now start honing your skills and guide your clients with the knowledge and intention you are creating in this workbook. …Lois

TABLE OF CONTENTS

Forward by Dr. Miller iii
A Note on How to Best Use This Book xii
Table of Contents xiii
Inductions / Selectivity 1
Evoking the Relaxation Response 3
Three to One Induction 5
Deepening the Trance State 7
Super Quick & Easy Induction 9
Instant Induction with Breath 11
Induction and Anchoring 13
Selective Awareness: Breath As an Induction 17
Safety Awareness 23

PRE-TALK & Patter 37

Deepening Phrases: Releasing Unhelpful Thoughts 49

Emerging Techniques 53
Basic Emerging 55
Count Up / Count Out 57
10 Great Emergings 61
Post Talk 77

Protocols for Spiritual Resources 79
Healing Resources 81
Empowering the Inner Healer 91
Empowering Healing Resources 99
Inner Connectedness 111
Processing Resources 123

APPENDIX 125
Imagination Exercises 127
Second Imagination Challenge 131
Third Imagination Challenge 133
Engaging Imagination 135
Putting It All Together Script 139

LEXICON of Hypnotic Terms and Phrases 161

SELECTIVITY EXERCISES

(Inductions)

Take a moment	*Utilization: Beginning break state*
And observe your experience of now…	*by observing outer / inner body*
Be aware of what you feel, physically…	*Fixation of Attention*
Be aware of what emotions you feel	*Content Suggestion*
Notice the temperatures that you feel	*Multi-Sensory Attention*
Warm parts of your body,	*Moves fixation quickly through the body*
Cool parts of your body,	*Apposition of Opposites*
Moist parts, dry	
The taste on your tongue	*Gustatory Awareness*
The fragrance in the air	*Olfactory Awareness*
The feeling of gravity	*Kinesthetic Awareness*
Drawing you downward,	*(voice pitch lowered on "down")*
Firmly into the surface beneath you.	*Creating Safety and Security*
Notice what thoughts	*Cognition*
Are going through your mind	
Notice what questions,	*Internal Musings*
What statements	*self- dialog is likely*
	to be going on right now
Or if none,	
Just notice the emptiness.	*Either way, all scenarios are covered!*
	A Pregnant pause here would be effective
Be aware of the position of your body	*Bypass Words to bypass*
As much as possible observing without	*conscious mental defense*
Doing anything without attempting to change it	
Simply accepting that experience	*Affirmation*
That is yours at this moment in time.	*Establishing Mindfulness*

EVOKING THE RELAXATION RESPONSE

Using what is going on in the listener's immediate environment is a wonderful way to induce trance state. Notice how Dr. Miller paces to the client's blink and complexion while implementing the following Utilization technique:

Just do whatever you can to relax,	*Client Centered, client in control*
Allowing your body be.	*Non-specific, other than to "be"*
Breathing in and out	*Pace this to the listener's breath*
And looking at that spot	*Fixation of Attention*
Breathing in and out	
Blinking a little more slowly	*Physically reflecting back to listener as blinking begins*
Body,	
Remains still.	
And the complexion of your face	
Is a little more red,	*Reflecting back what is happening*
And now eyes hardly blinking at all	*It's good to say hardly, because once attention is drawn to the eyes, there might be a natural blink or two*
And breathing out	*Pace and Lead listener's breath*
And then pausing,	
And another breath in,	*Listener is going to breathe anyway*
Deeper this time.	
And letting go	*Detachment / Dissociation*
Your hands gently relaxed	
(ie: on your abdomen)	*Outside Focus*
Another breath in …	*Fixation drawn inside...*
And out	
Good.	

THREE TO ONE INDUCTON

NB: If you are going to count the client down from three to one, please teach yourself to be consistent with counting DOWN to induce and Counting UP to bring Listener out of Hypnotic state.

Let your eyelids close.	*Direct Suggestion*
Good.	*Implying compliance and reassurance*
Notice how they gently close.	*Guiding a gentle closure to create hypnotic awareness*
Very, very deeply and comfortably relaxed.	*Somatic Response*
3. Releasing,	*Attach task to each number while listener is relaxing like rolling the head or letting legs move to a more comfortable position*
2. More relaxed.	*Deepening the release*
Good.	*Positive Reinforcement that Relaxation is occurring*
1. Down to the next level Allowing your mind to empty itself	*What is next level?* *Self-Permission to deeply relax letting go unnecessary thoughts*
And with this deep breath leaving Go all the way down to 0	*Upon exhalation of breath* *(Voice pitches down a bit)*
That's good.	*Reinforcement and Rapport*

DEEPENING THE TRANCE STATE

It's interesting how this can be an induction into trance state as well

In a moment	*Future Tense*
I'm going to count	
From three down to zero.	*Create Expectancy to deepen trance state*
Imagine there are four levels	*By-Pass Word*
And with each number	*Continuing Directions*
You will drift	*Reinforcing Expectancy*
To an even deeper level	
And when I reach the count of 0 you will be	*Concise instructions when trance will begin*
Very, very deeply and comfortably relaxed.	
3. Releasing,	*Once directions are clearly given then begin countdown*
Letting your legs	
Move to a more comfortable position,	*Attach some kind of desired behavior with each number*
2. Back more relaxed.	*Specifically direction awareness of locale*
Good.	*Implies success with directions*
1. Down to the next level	*Continuing to deepen trance state*
Allowing your mind to empty itself	
Of any unnecessary thoughts	
And with this deep breath leaving.	*Good use of exhalation to relax*
Go all the way down to 0	
That's good.	*Reassurance that listener is doing well*

Continue with your personalized suggestions for the listener as they are probably ready for the next level of trance state.

SUPER QUICK & EASY INDUCTION

This is not a first time process but is intended to be used with listener who has previously worked with you. Make sure they can reference to a Safe Space.

Let your eyelids close	*"To the Point" Authoritarian Suggestion* *The word "LET" makes it seem like it is client centered, doesn't it?*
And picture the word "relax"	*Listener has done this before. Even if listener is not visual, somehow, most seem to "get it"*
On the back of your forehead.	*Specific Attention of Fixation*
Think about that special place That you went to Or think of that image of yourself	*Cognitive Return to Safety* *Engaging imagination of success*
Really healthy and well.	
And sense again that word or phrase That came to you as a word Or anchor And say it to yourself now.	*Objectivity* *Reinforcement of former anchor word to create hypnotic state*
Let that happen if you're willing to now.	*Permissive Suggestion*

The Heart of Hypnosis & Deep Healing Workbook

INSTANT INDUCTION WITH BREATH

This is probably not the best first time induction for most listeners. You will want to create a bit more expectancy first. With that being said, I love using this with a rehearsed listener because it is quick and easy and works all the time!

Follow your breath
As it guides you to deeper relaxation.

>*Give the Listener ample opportunity to follow a cycle or two of their breath*

As the pause between breath
Gets longer and longer,

>*Pace your own breath to listener's breath cycle*

You go into hypnosis

>*Direct Command*

Deeper and deeper

>*I like the notion of "further and farther", (just individual preference and taste), and either phrase is quite successful*

Letting go
And falling into the Quiet Spot.

>*The whole concept of Letting Go is essential to inducing Hypnotic therapeutic state; And the notion of "Quiet Spot" is just the best example of initiating and deepening a trance simultaneously*

A longer version using breath and body scan to induce state is on the following page.

INDUCTION / ANCHORING

And perhaps you notice how gently	*Very permissive*
You have rolled your eyes up	*Using quick brainwave shift to induce*
Behind your closed eyelids.	*Keep directions clear: closed eyes*
And may you notice	*Directions of expectation*
A very gentle *fluttering feeling* of the eyelids.	*(If eyelids weren't fluttering before then, they may slightly flutter after suggestion)*

Breathing in, and as you let that breath out, *Compounding Relaxation*
Feel the letting go. *through breath*
Tuning into your awareness as you usually do *Turning Inward for trance*
And the deeper breath in,
Followed by an even deeper feeling   *Deep breath= letting go / release* Of letting go
  Compounding Suggestion

As you release it
And sink deeply into that pause *Exaggerating the pause between breath cycles enhances Relaxation*

And after this breath out
Really falling into that pause
Noticing the silence around you *(Make sure it is quiet)*
And hearing the sound of my voice *Fixation*
And in a moment I'm going to *Explaining what's about to happen*
Just press gently on your right forearm
And as I press gently on your right forearm, as I do,
Feel yourself falling even
More deeply into relaxation
(Pacing Head Movement / anchor) *Anchor—pressing gently on arm*
Gently falling to the side as your neck muscles relax
And now feel that greater relaxation of your neck muscles
Flow into the muscles of the shoulders as you let go.
Good ………..
A long pause like that allows you to drift very deep *Musing*
And to feel those subtle undulations *Feelings naturally experienced during trance*

That are kind of like waves. *Audio: Waves sound like Breathing = relaxing*

And perhaps that fluttering of your eyelids may go along *Causality*

With some colors that you see or seem to see. *Inner Hallucination*
Or perhaps there's just a feeling of *Internal /Digital: emotion / physical*
Releasing with each breath out. *Remember the Relaxation Response*
Good. *Implied success*

SELECTIVE AWARENESS:

BREATH AS AN INDUCTION

Allow yourself to center	*Immediately creating permission*
Which means to allow yourself to let go	*Explaining centering and mindfulness*
And be present in the present moment.	
Take a moment and be aware of your breathing,	*Deepening Technique: Breath happens in the moment as Listener breathes*
To be present and be aware of the fact	*Present + Aware = Mindfulness*
That this moment in time,	*THIS moment*
Is the only moment that exists.	
Every other moment that has ever been	*Past*
Is gone forever.	
Every moment that will be	*Future*
Is completely unknowable right now	
But this moment exists;	*Reinforce notion of the moment*
You're breathing is a way to get into that moment,	*Breath = Awareness*
Just be in touch with your breathing,	*Kinesthetic / Sensory input:*
Feel the coolness of the air	*Opposite feelings: cool/warm*
As it enters your nostrils	*Pace to Listener's breath*
Feel the warmth as it leaves.	
Feel the release that comes with each breath out.	
Feel the energy that starts with each new breath in.	*Using breath to induce state reviving energy*
Notice how deeply or how shallowly you breathe	*Observation and*
Without having to change it.	*acceptance of the moment*
Just be in touch with it.	
It begins with *awareness*.	*Premise to all change and healing*
The idea is to experience it without interfering,	*Teaching mindfulness*
Just observing,	
As if you were a guest here in this body.	*And isn't that the truth!*
And as you get to that place of in a sense,	

Being the observer of what's going on	
We call that centering.	*Observer = Centering*
Just being focused within	*Turning to the Inner World*
And observing.	
And allow the experience to happen.	*Permissive, Client Centered*

If you wanted to continue to hypnotic experience, the following extension to the preceding induction explains Selective Awareness to Listener. Deliver this rather quickly….

There are always two levels operating,	*Deepening / Educating*
That which we are conscious of	
And that which we have not yet	
Become conscious of.	
Now think about an apple.	*The moment each word is spoken, images represent words appear in listener's mind:*
Think about a *mountain*,	
Think about the *big toe* on your *right foot*,	
Become aware of the *tip of the tongue*,	
Become aware of your *eyelids*,	
Notice if they are *open* or *closed*,	
Still or moving.	*Apposition of Opposites*
Notice which phrase of your breathing	
You are in right now.	
Feel your clothing where it touches your body.	*Tactile Awareness*
Think about the *Eiffel tower*,	*Image Awareness*
Think about a *sailboat*,	
Think about a *jack in the box*,	
Think about a *jack o lantern*.	
Become aware of the *sound of my voice*	*Bring back voice awareness*
And the feeling of your	
Little *finger* on your left hand.	*Awareness of body*
Really not a problem.	*Musing*
Now, think of all of them at the same time and you can't.	*Convincer*
The interesting thing about our mind then	*Musing*

At a conscious level,	
There's an almost infinite number of things	Mind = Infinite
That we can be conscious of,	
But at any given moment,	
We can only become conscious of one thing at a time.	Realization
That's what we call Selective Awareness.	Defines Selective Awareness
Who chooses what you are aware of in the moment?	Interesting passage
Most of us go through life being aware	moves from <u>you</u> to <u>us</u> to <u>we</u> to <u>I</u>
Of whatever we're aware of	
Without ever thinking of what	
I am thinking about that.	Confusion to ractionate trance state
What is the effect of that thought	
On my mind?	Different levels of Mind work synergistically
Is that thought leading me	Musing Choice at the Deepest Level
Toward a creative approach	
Of my life?	
Or is it leading me toward	Or, *will this* OR *that happen?*
A defensive approach of my life?	*Establishing Personal Values:*
Enhancing my life or my relationship?	
We never think about that.	
When we do,	Result of OR
We become more able	
To use our Selective Awareness.	Desired Outcome
What you are making conscious,	Re-prompting visual images
Even though you're not thinking about it,	
Your subconscious mind	
Still has the Eiffel tower,	Repetition
Jack-o-lantern, all waiting	
For you to reach in and grab it and be aware.	
It's selecting all of these things to be aware of	Choice and
And follow in a certain pathway.	Action
What is the pathway	
You cut with your mind?	Metaphor to "clear the way"

SAFETY AWARENESS

Safety brings an enormous value to entering the doorway into the deeper mind. Increased continuing rapport with the listener allows the person to feel safe.

Be aware	*Beginning Mindfulness*
That there is always a deep state of relaxation	
That is within you.	
And when you become distracted	
By the outside world	
Or when you become distracted by thoughts	
About the outside world	*Dissociative Confusion Induction*
Or about the past or about the future	*Creating Time Distortion*
You may forget	*Creating Amnesia*
That this relaxation is always within you	*Accessing Recollection of past Tension Incidents: used as comparative resource*
Just as the stars are still there in the daytime	*Truism: reversed AS / THIS*
So too this relaxation is always within you	*Cause & Effect*
And as you let go of the thoughts	*Dissociation / Detachment*
The mental tensions	*Mentally*
And *as you* let go of the tightness in your body,	*& Physically*
The physical tensions	*Bridging: As you… then your Awareness is able to…*
Then your awareness	*Heightened awareness of inner experience*
Is able to perceive that relaxation within	*When Deeper Mind is relaxed, new ways of healing or problem solving occurs*
So, by being aware of this,	*Same as "therefore" logic*
And giving yourself permission to be present	*Grounding in the moment*
To let go of the past or the future	*Detachment / Dissociation*
To let go of the questions;	*Stepping away from Conscious Mind*
And then take a deep breath in and as	*Breathing Reflex*
You let it out, think or picture the word relax	*Reinforcing Relaxation with the Healing Experience*

As you very, very gently	*This action initiates shift in brainwave pattern*
Allow your eyes to roll upward	*to induce hypnoidal state*
Only as much as is comfortable	*Maintaining safety and comfort*
Behind your closed eyelids.	*(Good to add to insure listener keep eyes closed while performing this task)*
Picture the word RELAX	*Listener has choice of which to image: the word or the scene; either way, Listener sends self relaxation message*
Or picture that relaxing scene	*Double Bind*
That you chose to look at	
A little while ago	*Assessing previously visualized relaxation*
And think to yourself	*Inner Access of suggestion*
That word or phrase that you found	*This becomes a key word or image*
That represents	*to associate with following suggestion:*
Relaxation,	
Peace, calm...	*Activating previously obtained Anchor, Cue or Post Hypnotic of Peace and Calm*
Let your eyelid muscles relax to the point	*Small Muscle Catalepsy*
They feel like they just don't want to open,	*Convincer*
And as you have that feeling of relaxation in your eyelids	
And as you very gently test them and as you test them	*Bypassing Critical Factor of Mind*
Let that relaxation flow through your body.	*to allow relaxation*
And as you *test them*	*Challenge to Convince*
Let this relaxation	*with resulting physical relaxation*
Flow down through your body	*Head to toe release*
And as you *test them* again	*Convincer; listener is in control*
Even more gently	*Deepening / Repetition*
Allow even more relaxation	*Allowance keeps client in control of the experience*
And a more subtle feeling of relaxation	
And as you *test them*	*By this time, listener is convinced of relaxation*

Let this relaxation	
Flow down through your body	*Flowing Downward to enhance release*
As it reaches your fingertips	*Creates awareness of relaxation location*
Take a deep breath in	*And tasking Listener with more tasks*
Draw it up into the center of your chest,	*(Pace to Listener's breath cycle)*
Letting it out.	*Deliver upon exhalation*
And as you feel your chest relax,	*Guiding Relaxation with suggestion*
Let yourself sink deeply into that Pause.	*Wait for the space between exhalation and inhalation*
After you breathe out	*(Continue Pacing with breath)*
And before the next breath comes in.	
And feel your chest and your abdomen relax,	*Downward Body Scan*
Let it flow down through your pelvis and your thighs	
And your knees and your legs and your feet	
All the way down to the very tips of your toes	*Listener is relaxed by now*
And at anytime any unnecessary thoughts come along	*Mental Release*
You may erase those unnecessary thoughts	*"Erasing' is a metaphor Dr. Miller often uses*
From your mind.	
This is your mind and it belongs to you.	*Trance Logic—Ego Enhancement*
And you have the right	*Permissive, ego-strengthening*
And the power	
To let go of any thoughts	*Detaching from "unserving, unnecessary" thoughts*
That are not serving you;	
Unnecessary thoughts	
Release them,	
Erase them from your mental blackboard	*Highly visual and kinesthetic*
And as you test *them*	*Subconscious Reference to eyelids*
Let this relaxation	*Eyelid Catalepsy begins ; moving down the body creating large motor lethargy*
Flow down through your body	
And as you *test them* again	*With each "test" convincer, trance is fractionated / deepened*
Even more gently	*Always maintaining safety for listener*

Allow even more relaxation	*Self-Permission*
And a more subtle feeling of relaxation to	
Flow through all the muscles of your face,	*Progressive Relaxation*
Your jaw, your neck and shoulders,	*Descending Body Scan*
Your arms and hands	
Down to your fingertips.	
And if that same thought	*Unnecessary = Unserving*
Or any other thought comes along,	
That's unnecessary	
Just erase it.	*Erase / Deletion*
	of unnecessary thoughts
Unnecessary thoughts or thoughts	
About the past or the future,	*Creating Mindfulness of NOW*
Questions, doubts, comparisons,	
Judgments, criticisms,	
Unneeded right now.	
Allow yourself just to be here.	*Permission to experience Mindfulness*
Experience the stillness	*("Be still, and know that you are God")*
As you sink deeply into that *pause*	*The Point where the cycle of*
	breath is most relaxed
After you breathe out	
And before you breathe in again,	*Process Imagery:*
	Coming into the present moment
The quietest time of all	
For all your mind and body.	
And as you *touch this place within*	*Emotional: Inner Kinesthetic*
Allow yourself to just flow through time	
And space a little ways	*Time Travel:*
	Accessing Reference Memory
To a time in that past that represents	
Inspiration to you.	
A time perhaps when you felt *love*	*Guiding images of past inspiration:*
Maybe a time when you felt in *deep communication*	
With that *Spirit* that moves though all things.	

A *sacred moment*, a *holy* moment,
A moment of revelation,
An *epiphany*,
Or just a time of just *feeling secure*, Whole.

That time when the *essence of you*   *Thinker of the Thought*
Felt most at peace or most empowered.   *Creates scenario for healing*
And see what recollection comes to you.   *(Pause for a moment:*
what may seem to be a long time
to you may seem short
in the subconscious state)

It could be something
From just a little while ago,   *Creating Timeline*
Minutes or hours ago   *regressing to inspiring time*

Could be days weeks or years,
It could be something from your childhood
Let yourself float to that place
As if you are riding on a *magic carpet*   *A familiar metaphor for Dr. Miller*
And bring it to mind   *Retrieve the Memory by*

Either picture it in your mind   *accessing Visual Memory*
Or hear the sounds.   *accessing Auditory Memory*
Feel yourself *touching*   *accessing Kinesthetic Memory*
That experience within you   *and all sensory images*
Use all the senses that you can
See, feel touch, hear, smell, touch,   *Synthesia*
But most of all,
Let yourself feel the sense   *Feeling empowered*
Of empowerment,   *creates empowerment*

Of wholeness,
Of a connection,
With something greater than just yourself,
Perhaps.   *Keeps suggestion Permissive*
And allow yourself to feel the reality of

That.	Referring to empowerment, wholeness and connection to something greater than oneself
And to notice where you feel it in your body.	This "feeling" confirms the self-empowerment is real
Maybe you feel it just a *little bit*	Double bind through comparisons assuming Listener is feeling empowered
Or maybe you feel it *strongly*.	
And as you breathe into it let *it grow stronger*.	ie: Self Empowerment
Breathe into that place within you	
Where you feel that feeling.	Identifying where feeling lies
And as you breathe into it let it grow stronger	
Maybe it is a sense of knowing	Prompting potential
That there are extraordinary possibilities within you,	
And that you have a purpose for being here	Prompting purpose
And that purpose has something to do with	
Healing in some way…	
And imagine that you can trust in this	
Deeper place within you	Indirect Suggestion
And the sense of connection	
That something is greater than you,	
A sense of connection with people,	
Or however it might form itself for you	Opens Listener imagination
Imagine that you can allow this place within you	
This quality, this *feeling*	Kinesthetic
This sense, to guide you	
And as *you reflect back*	Indirect Future Pacing:
On the things that moved you today,	
the things you touched upon	Inner Digital Learning
Imagine that that deeper sense of Spirit	
Or empowerment	
Or of essence	
Can empower you to use those experiences	
To heal yourself and those that you serve.	Not "help" but "serve"

Reflect back over the things that moved you today.　　　　　　　　　　*By-pass word*
And let it　　　　　　　　　　　　　　　　　　　　　　　　　　　　*Process Imagery:*
　　　　　　　　　　　　　　　　　　　　　　　　　　　　　　　Intensifying and
　　　　　　　　　　　　　　　　　　　　　　　　　　　　generalizing Awareness

Spill out to every other cell of your body.

Pregnant Pause　　　　　　　　　　　　　　　　　　*(Gives listener time to reflect and*
　　　　　　　　　　　　　　　　　　　　　process on a cellular, healing level)

PRETALK

Preparing Listener for the Therapeutic Procedure

Pre Talk is a very important ingredient in any good hypnosis protocol. Forgetting to do a pre-talk is like icing an unbaked cake. Before guiding listener into hypnosis, always get permission from listener first. Safety First!

Would you like to learn how to relax deeply and by relaxing be able to get to a state of mind where you can solves the problem that you came to see me about? *This is the consensual agreement between client and therapist*

I wonder if you'd like to sit down and relax and be present...I wonder if you'd like for me to show you a way to be more calm and comfortable.
Very permissive style of induction

	style of induction
Before we begin let's just take a few moments	
To relax and be present	*Begin Centering*
Making a transition from one state of consciousness	*Creating Expectation of Hypnosis*
Such as the one that you needed on the highway	*Duality & Comparison*
To drive you here;	
To the state of consciousness	
That will help you learn the most from this today	*Assuming there will be knowledge*
To get the most out of what we're doing here today.	*Result Orientated*
To go through this procedure with the	
Most relaxation	*Comparative: The Most /*
And the least discomfort.	*The Least*
Relax and allow yourself to make that transition	*Relax = transition*
Making those transitions	
Are really important in life	*Easing transitions of everyday life*
If you look at those things cause stress for us	

It is making changes.	*The need to Pause and Center:*
Getting up in the morning and getting out to school	*Time Distortion to*
Or beginning work or at the beginning of the day	*deepen induction*
Or at the end of a vacation or packing for a trip;	*Confusion Technique*
All of these transitions.	
Once you've been there for a while you can relax.	

So just take a deep breath in
And you let that breath out   *Begin de-stressing listener*
And as you let that breath out
Allow your eyelids to close   *Permissive (Maternal) suggestion style*

And think to yourself the word,   *The Thought brings on the relaxation*
Relax.   *Relaxation allows opening to wisdom and spirituality*
Let yourself be aware   *Permissive Suggestion*
That there is no other place you have to go   *Leading: Relaxation*
There is no task you need to perform   *Permission to break state*
Nothing you need to figure out.   *A Conscious Mind can check out*
    There's nothing else you need to do.
Your body therefore can be completely at rest,   *Body is at rest*
Completely at ease   *Ease*
Your mind can be at ease   *Repeated Ease in Mind*
    And your emotions can relax
    Relax Emotions

Allow all tension
And all anxiety to flow out of your body
And allow all unnecessary thoughts
To flow out of your mind
And allow yourself to be here.   *Becoming Present*
And from this place
Briefly, picture yourself coming here today.   *Regressing to recent images*
Remember how you got here,
Remember coming into this room,
Remember how you got yourself to the seat you are in now.
Take another deep breath   *Break State*
And as you let it out

Think the words,	*Auditory Imagery*
Here and now	*Accessing Resources at deepest Sense of Self*
And if you are willing to do so,	*Tasking the listener*
Think to yourself, I give myself permission to be present	*Mindfulness*

And here at this present moment in time,	*Mindfulness*
Just becoming aware of who you are	*Spiritual Resource: Self Awareness*
At the deepest level	
Beyond what ever job you may have	*Listener is more than the job*
Whatever social roles you may play	*or social role or relationships or*
Whatever relationships you may be in	*hobbies or body*
Whatever profession,	
Whatever hobby you may do,	
Whatever your physical condition may be	
At this moment in time	
Deeper than all those things.	*Assignment of Value*

Go to your deepest sense of who you are	*Accessing future pacing of Spiritual Resources*

And think to yourself,
  I am.   *"I AM" is the sound or name for God in many cultures*
                                               Whatever words you say after I Am creates your truth

I am.	*Reinforcement and Repetition*
And if you have a word for it	
Such as I am Love or	*"I am" Auditory autosuggestion*
I am part of a healing	
I am a spirit	
I am a child of God	
I am at peace	
I am	
Think it.	
Let all other thoughts	*Maintaining trance state through mental release*
Just fade away…	*(Remember to pause for a moment here)*

And just allow yourself to appreciate	*Self-Appreciation*
This deepest sense of who you are	*Gratitude*
Realizing that at this point	

You are not yet perfect
And you aren't supposed to be.   *Self-Forgiveness*

Realize that that deepest level
You are committed to grow   *Understanding Potential of Self*
More and more
Into your true self   *Something greater than what we think we are*
So that who you are
Expresses itself   *Establishes High Self-Regard*
More completely in every thought,
Every word,
Every action.
Just be aware of that.   *It's good to point out things to the*
                                  Subconscious Mind to reinforce your point!

Good.   *Reassurance*
 And become aware of your sense of   *Accessing Healing Resource*
What true healing is
Perhaps by *reflecting* at time   *Inner Audio-digital suggestion/Regression*
Where you've seen dramatic   *Visual proof of healing*
Instances of true healing,   *about to define range of healing:*

Whether that be a birth, Marriage
Success in life,   *Good trance word to use consistently*

Physical healing
Emotional healing
Or even healing into old age or the end of life
Reflect upon that,   *Audio-digital reinforced*
Your sense of what healing is.   *Personalization*

Understand that you may not have
A perfect and complete knowledge yet
    In life of all that healing is   *Life is a Process*
Simply allow yourself   *Keeps client safe and in control*
To allow yourself to be   *Mindfulness*
That which you are aware of
Even if you don't have words for it,

Because the meaning goes deeper than words.	*Trance Logic*
Perhaps it comes as an image	*Guided images*
Of a particular event of a	
Family member or situation	*Person, Place or Thing*
Perhaps it's a kinesthetic quality within your body	
Perhaps an emotional tone that comes to you	
Or perhaps it comes in some other sense	
That has no name.	*Reflecting on Past to be more Present in the Now: Presence empowers Choice*
Be in touch with what you healing is	*Kinesthetic self-connection*
At this time, now.	*Mindfulness reinforced*
And reflect upon your experiences yesterday	*Regress to recent event*
And what there was that happened	*for more Resources*
That maybe helping you to become	
Even more aware	
Of who you are	
And of what you can do	*Task self-empowerment through self-healing*
To help facilitate	
Healing in whatever area	
Within yourself, or others,	*Personal to Local to Global Healing*
Or in the world around you.	
What touched you yesterday?	*Musings to create problem solving resources*
What did you allow to move you?	*Bridging resource -past to future*
What new perspectives,	*Implying there <u>are</u> new perspectives*
What new ideas	*and new strategies and ideas*
Can you at this moment recall,	
Easily.	
Let them come to you as they will.	*It's o.k. to take your time*

The deeper mind is thinking hundreds,
Thousands of times more

Then you are at the conscious level. *Reinforces processing information without conscious involvement: Implies Listener has a good ally with subconscious mind that continues to work constantly, whether one is conscious of it or not*

EMERGE

DEEPENING PHRASES:

To Release Unhelpful Thoughts

1. Are you willing to let go of that belief?
    We already possess what it is we need in side.
   The healing is already here, present,
   Hypnosis is, peace, love, life is already here.
    But we might be unaware of it
   And can't use what we have.
   We're lost.
    We have compasses in our pockets,
   But forget to put our hands in our pockets.

2. We spend so much time looking outside of ourselves,
   When we already have it inside!
    Let's hide THE TRUTH inside,
   They'll never think of looking for it there."

3. The Cause of all suffering is wanting things
   To be different from how they actually are!
    We can accept things are they are at this moment,
   Without judgment, without criticism.

4. Things are as they are.
    They can't be any different.
    Everything had to happen exactly as it had to happen.
    From all we can tell, the reason you're here
   Is because you got in the car.

   (Keep this relevant to listener)

5. The past is over.
    Only this moment in time exists:
   Acceptance of things as they are.
    The past is over.
    God wrote the past precisely as it is.
    So, I don't have to be ashamed,

Guilty,
Feel criticized about it,
Feel bad about it.

6. No need to feel angry or worried
   Or sad about it so,
   I have all of my faculties available to me NOW,
   Instead half of my mind worried about
   (i.e.: what I said to my mother,
   Or another half feeling sad about my dead dog)
   Or what's going to happen next week,
   And what is the price of gold.

7. So, you can be as creative
   With what is existing in this moment,
   Here and now.

8. Reflecting on the Past
   In order to become more Present
   In the Now
   With an ability to choose differently

9. Presence empowers Choice

10. Choosing at the deepest level:
    Regarding Personal Values,
    What will serve you best,
    What actions can you choose
    To produce the outcomes
    You want in the future?
       What has heart and meaning for you?   *Future Pacing: Future Projection of Listener's deepest Desires*

EMERGING TECHNIQUES

BASIC EMERGING

If you guide Listener into hypnosis, it is your duty to guide them out of it as well. Disengagement, Emerging, De-hypnotization, Count-out, Disengagement, Ending Trance, Return to Awareness, Coming Back and THE RETURN are all terms and phrases that tell the listener this particular hypnotic experience has come to an end and is over. Dr. Miller skillfully provides some great emerging statements, always leaving the listener refreshed and returning with good positive feelings.

There are remarkable similarities with the following emerging and the Serenity Prayer, both fabulous vehicles of thought. You might do yourself and your client a favor if you were to memorize this emerging phrase.

And when you relax in this way,	*Trance Logic / Causality*
It allows you to accept those things	*Permission to Regain Control*
That you wish to accept,	
Will allow you to act	*Outcome Imagery of desired success*
With more commitment	
And power	
To change the things that you really	
Want to change.	
It will allow you to accept with serenity	
Those things that you know	
It is wise to accept.	
And the inner experiences	
That you have when you are relaxed,	
Will lead you to ever deeper levels	
Of understanding and wisdom	
Concerning yourself,	
The world around you…	
And take you to a place of true peace,	*Serenity comes with peace*
Love and freedom,	
If you wish.	*What is better than self healing and personal growth, peace, love, and freedom?*

COUNT UP

This is a simple way to bring client out of state. Don't forget to brighten your voice and quicken the tempo as you bring them back to outside awareness. And stay consistent! DO NOT count down to induce AND emerge the Listener. Count DOWN to induce and always, always, always count up to emerge. The following is a wonderful example of a quick efficient Return.

And in a moment,
          Creating Expectancy

I'm going to count from one to three   *Using simple clear directions*
And as I do, I'm going to ask that you   *Tasking listener*
Let yourself come all the way back
To being alert and aware of where you are.
Your eyes will open   *Creating clear directions*
And you'll feel refreshed,
Rested and clear.

One, coming up   *Coming UP / Count UP*

Two, light and lighter   *The best Imagery to return to is to create a notion of Light-ness*

And more and more alert,
More and more *awake*.   *Would "consciously aware" work also?*

Three, as I touch your arm, your eyelids open,   *You may discover, it's not necessary to touch the arm to emerge client.*
Wide awake.   *Awake implies that the listener has been sleeping; we explained earlier that hypnosis is NOT sleep, maybe alert, aware and refreshed might work too*
Good.   *Positive Feedback*
Take a moment and just notice how comfortable you feel.
   This is important insure a good experience for the Listener upon emerging.

Good.

What was that like for you? *I also like to ask Listener what stands out most in their mind? What memory do they bring forward from the experience? What message do you have for yourself? Then, sit back allowing them to verbalize. Listen to their messages*

10 GREAT EMERGINGS

These could be used separately or combined as a very long Return

EMERGING 1: And bringing yourself completely back
Into this moment of time, now
Imagine simply allowing yourself to *open*
As fully and completely as you are willing to
To allow yourself to
Learn whatever is of value to you
To open your mind to be flexible to new perspectives
To be willing to experiment with those, internally
In conversations with yourself
In your work with others.
Imagine your mind *open* like a chalice,
To receive, from me, from the others
Or from that spirit that moves through all things.

EMERGING 2: And take a deep breath in and as you let it out
Simply allow yourself *to settle*
Feelings of gratitude toward the source of all these things
And take a deep breath in and as you let it out
Let those thoughts go and
Allow yourself simply *to settle*
With gratitude to the Source
From all these things.
And once again in touch with yourself
At the deepest level,
Gradually begin to allow yourself to come
Back in your own time in your own speed.

EMERGING 3: When you're ready,
Letting yourself breathe a little more deeply
Letting your arms stretch
Coming all the way up.
Allowing your eyelids to open.
Wide awake.

And again, take a moment and reflect upon
How you feel now
And upon this experience you've just allowed yourself.

EMERGING 4: This is a different moment now.
This is a new world that's never happened before.
This is a new you.
You never step into the same river twice…
You never see the same flower twice,
You never breathe the same breath twice.

Be yourself now
As you emerge into this new moment,
A completely new person,
Filled with new possibilities
Wherever your ability to choose.
Allowing yourself coming back fully
And be prepared to pilot yourself safely and steadily
Through the course of your experience here.

EMERGING 5: Clearing your mind,
Putting this information in a file,
Or storing a book,
Or set it aside to be present
As today you made some important steps forward
And you'll be able to continue this at home,
And for now,
Let's continue to use your ability
To adjust your emotions and behavior
And state of mind by coming back
To being relaxed and comfortable,
In a state of mind allowing you
To deal effectively what you need to deal with
Until it's the right time to deal with this again.
Set it aside and come back to it later.

EMERGING 6:   Now, gradually
   Allow yourself to return back to this place
   Where you are seated in this room.
   Sense the position of your body,
   Feel its relaxation
   Be aware of the day
   Be aware of what you are doing here
   Almost as though you were taking a little nap,
   As if you were on a little journey.

   And now you are returning back
   Gradually re-awakening.
   Letting your body begin to stretch and move a little bit.
   Coming all the way back,
   Breathing a little more deeply
   Maybe stretching your neck and your head,
   Your shoulders, feet or your fingers.
   Come all the way back.
   And when you're ready
   Take a deep breath in and
   As you let that breath out,
   And your eyelids open
   And just think to yourself,
   Wide awake and present
   Here and now.
   Good.

EMERGING 7:   Sense what you've gained from this experience
   And know that these gains are with you forever…
   And then perhaps you can already begin to imagine
   Some ways of using these skills in your own life
   In your own healing
   And perhaps you can picture that or think about it
   Or wonder
   Let it happen.
   Allow yourself this positive fantasy.
   Remember, the future is not someplace…
   The future is a place we are creating.

And we create it
With each emotion
With each word and with each action.
Hold in mind an image of that,
That you wish to create.
Something that gives your life
Meaning and value.

Each time you picture yourself the
Way you really want to be
You have become a person because
You are already the person you want to be
Down deep inside
More and more how to let go of any obstacles.
You're able to express more and more
Your own essence.

And then as you bring yourself back to being wide-awake,
You can bring back with you these images and beliefs,
Feelings as you wish.
So as I count from one to three
Allow yourself to come back,
And although you have been awake all the time,
Shift your state…

EMERGING 8: And imagine how the world could begin
To transform a little bit more
If what you know,
Of what you feel,
Could spread out.
Imagine yourself kind of like
An antenna or light bulb
And imagine that you could
Radiate this quality
Effortlessly,   *Easily is a clearer word or*
Without trying   *image to subconscious.*
Without acting, in any particular way,
Just being.

Imagine that as you relax
And allow yourself simply to be;
To center.

You are able to see more clearly
And that something is ignited within you.
As you see and as you understand
Something radiates out from this center;
Maybe you have a name for it, maybe not
Maybe you have a color for it, maybe not,
Or a sound,
Or maybe it's a kind of music,
Or a touch or feeling,
And imagine that as you go forth from this point now
That you continue to be a Radiant Being.

And as you go forth,
Visualize yourself using some of the perspectives
You have gained here today…
Return to an awareness of the outside,
And yet feeling clear,
More confidence,
Balanced feeling inside,
And returning back into this room,
Coming up into this moment, eyelids open…

EMERGING 9: You are really free to connect
In a whole new way,
Peaceful and
Discovering a new kind of joy and freedom and wholeness.
Let your 'yes finger' move
When you can imagine that. *Ideomotor communication*
Good.
You remain *in touch* with these feelings
And each time you listen to this process *Post Hypnotic Suggestion*
Any time you listen to this process,
You can return to this experience *Makes it easier to return to state*

With all these awareness you have right now.
And in fact, any time you wish,
Anytime the going gets rough,
Any time you begin to feel (   )   *(State listener's desired outcome)*
That in the past might have pulled you off course
With (- whatever issue -   ),
You can immediately stop, and go within
To this present moment., and relax.
Touch your deeper self, know the Truth
And to remember all those things
That you have just allowed yourself to learn.
And then after a few moments of relaxing in this way
Then you return to become
Much more wide awake,   *(Dehypnotization)*
Much more willing to make the choices
The decisions that are right for you.
And in a similar way
I'm going to ask you now to let yourself
Return back to an awareness of the outside
And yet perhaps with a feeling
Of being different in a certain way,
Clearer, more centered more confident, more comfortable.
And as you are coming,
Keeping the balanced feeling in side
Aware of yourself
Returning back to this room
Coming back to this moment
Where your eyelids open
Taking a moment to see how you feel.

EMERGING 10: *I've added more comments to this final Emerging for you*

And *reflect* upon your experiences yesterday   *Bypass word*
Of what happened yesterday   *Recalling positive resources*
                                                       from recent memory

To become even more
Of who you are   *Ego enhancement*
Of what you can do to help

Facilitate healing in whatever area	
In yourself	*Healing is Personalized*
In others	*Local / community healing*
In the world	*Global healing*
In whatever *(keep personalized for listener)......*	
What touched you yesterday?	*Re-connecting to feelings / emotional state*
What did you allow to move you?	*Choice; Self Permission*
What new ideas can you at this moment	*How can something new be easily recalled? Trance logic going on* Recall, easily?
Just letting them come to you as you will.	*Permissive*
Your deeper mind is working, hundreds even	*Deeper Mind*
Thousands of times at a conscious level	*is powerful*
And bringing yourself back	*Creating awareness of return*
In to this moment of time	*to the present time*
Now	
Allowing yourself to open	*Permissive Suggestion of acceptance*
As fully and as completely	*Client centered suggestion*
As you are willing to.	*keeps client in control*
To allow yourself to learn	*Tasking client with self-permission to*
Whatever it is of value to you	*take what they need from the experience*
Imagine your mind open	*Metaphor:*
Like a chalice	*Mind is precious like a chalice*
To receive from me	*Listener is the Recipient; Beneficiary*
And from that spirit	*This is also a Navajo concept of Spirit*
That moves through all things.	
And take a deep breath in	*Allow listener to fill lungs / model*
And as you let it out	*(Exhale as you deliver this line)*
Let all of those thoughts go.	*Thoughts are released as breath releases*
Simply allow yourself	*Easy to give self permission*
To settle into the	
Source of all these things.	*To be part of Source*

And once again, at the deepest level,	*Emergence begins*
Allow yourself	*Easy, simple return; don't rush it*
Gradually	
In your own time	
And in your own speed	
When you're ready	
Letting yourself breathe a bit more deeply	*Watch for listener's deep breath in response to the suggestion*
Let your arms stretch and move	*Watch them respond physically*
Coming all the way up.	
Allowing your eyelids to open *wide awake*;	*(or, fully alert)*
In your own time,	
And take a moment and reflect	
On what just happened.	*Provides post-talk opportunity*

POST - TALK

This is a very important part of the hypnotic experience, as the listener probably is in a light trance state upon opening eyes. Reinforcement of what occurred during the experience is essential to a good experience for the listener.

And take a moment and	*Maintaining hypnotic suggestion language*
And Notice how comfortable you feel	*Always make sure listener returns feeling great*
And reflect upon that experience.	*Give listener a moment to do this*
Recalling for a moment	*Conscious Review Each of the steps of relaxation of hypnotic experience*
And going to your special place	*Step 1*
Visualizing yourself healthy and well	*Step 2*
Being in touch with the deepest part of you	*Step 3*

And recall what word or phrase came to you, if any.

How long does that experience seem to you?	*Trance Ratification: proves trance existed: TIME DISTORTION; 30 minutes Could have felt like 10 minutes to one listener and like an hour to another*

SPIRITUAL RESOURCES

SPECIAL RESOURCES

HEALING RESOURCES

And as you allow your eyelids to close	*Begins the inward journey*
Think to yourself, the word relax	*Inner Audio keyword: Relax*
And become aware that at this moment in time	*Strategy:*
There is no other place that you have to go.	*Permission to be hypnotized*
There's no task that you need to perform,	
There's nothing else you need to do.	
The body therefore can be completely relaxed,	*Relaxation is key to Deep Healing; although hypnosis is NOT relaxation, it is necessary to break spasm of pain cycle*
Completely at ease.	
And your mind can be at ease	*Integration of body and mind*
And your emotions can relax.	*and emotional Being*
Allow all tension and all anxiety to flow	
Out of your body	
Allow all unnecessary thoughts to flow	
Out of your mind	
And allow yourself to be here	*Creating Mindfulness*
And from this place,	*Assumes Listener is in this place*
Briefly, picture yourself coming here today	*Opening Memory Retrieval*
Remember how you got here.	*Regressive Suggestion*
Remember coming into this room.	
Remember how you got yourself to the seat you are in now.	
And as you breathe in	*Redirects focus to breath cycle as*
And as you let it out	*a confusion technique to induce hypnotized state*
Think the words,	*Internal audio suggestion*
Here and now.	*MINDFULNESS*
And if you are willing to do so,	*Permissive Style to Task Listener*
think to yourself the words,	*Direct thought that changes from*
I give myself permission to be present	*third person to first person Subconscious mind will be aware of what is being said and understands the intention of words*
And here at this present moment in time	*MINDFULNESS*

Just becoming aware of who you are	*Becoming the Observer*
At the deepest level,	
Beyond whatever job you may have,	
Whatever social role you may play,	
Whatever relationship / s you may be in,	
Whatever profession,	
Whatever hobby you may do,	
Whatever your physical condition	
May be at this moment at time;	
Deeper than all those things	
Go to your deepest sense of who you are	*Jung called this the Thinker of the Thought*
And think to yourself the words	
I am.	
I am.	*Repetition to deepen the notion of Be-ing*
And if you have a word for it	*Formulating abstract thought into symbol*
Such as I am Love,	*Gentle leading and Guidance by Speaker*
Or I am part of a healing,	
I am a spirit.	
I am a child of God.	
I am at peace,	
I am.	*Repetition and reinforcement*
Think it.	*Direct Suggestion to Internalize*
Let all other thoughts just fade away	*You may desire to take a brief pause here to dramatize the time for the thoughts to fade away. This also creates a bit of time distortion*
And just allow yourself to *appreciate*,	*Keyword: appreciation*
Realizing that at this point	*Awareness in this moment*
You are not yet perfect	*Subconscious hears this as "You are perfect"*
And you're not supposed to be.	
You are committed to continue	*Without commitment and action there can be no change*
To grow more and more	*Growth implies change*
Into your true self	*True self is what most seek*

So that who you are expresses itself	
More completely.	*Self-Actualization that comes with*
Every thought,	*Word and Deed*
Every word,	
Every action,	
Just be aware of that.	
Good.	*Assuring client that they are aware of "that"*
And become aware of your	*Inner Digital process/Aware; Sense*
Of what true healing is	*Healing Sensory Awareness is Listener's own creation of feelings.*
Perhaps by *reflecting* upon at times	*Reflection: Inner Digital process thoughtful and pensive*
When you've seen as	*Creating Visual Resource*
Important instances of	
Healing	
Whether that healing be of birth	
Marriage	
Success in life	
Physical healing	
Emotional healing	
Or healing into old age or	
At the end of life	
Reflect upon that,	*Reinforcement of Suggestion to heighten listener's Visual Recall; Future Projection of Healing experiences*
Your sense of what healing is.	
Understanding that you may not have a perfect	*Again to the Subconscious Awareness, the message is*
And complete knowledge yet	*"You have a perfect, complete knowledge of all that healing is"*
Of all that healing is.	
Simply allow yourself to allow yourself	*Allow to Allow is great languaging; client centered, safe and effective!*

Completely	*This word implies fulfillment, totality*
That which you are aware of	*Awareness refers to the Subconscious Awareness*
Even if you don't have words for it	
Because the meaning goes deeper than words	*Words prompt symbols, pictures or images to the Subconscious Mind; implying that this is a special important experience of healing: i.e., beyond words*
Perhaps it comes as an image,	*Guiding Listener to more Visual Resources*
Or a particular event or person	
Or family or situation,	
Perhaps it's a kinesthetic feeling,	*Feeling Resource*
A quality within your body,	*(Physical)*
Perhaps it's an emotional tone.	*(Emotional)*
Or perhaps it comes in some other sense	*(Open Ended)*
That has no name	
Be in touch	*Kinesthetic awareness of healing*
With your notion of what your healing is	
At this time.	*Now: Mindfulness*
And reflect upon your experiences yesterday	*Regress to Resource*
And what there was that happened	
That maybe helping you to become	
Even more aware	
Of who you are	*(I wonder, do YOU know who you are?)*
And of what you can do	
To help facilitate	
Healing in whatever area	
Within yourself,	*Beginning a common theme of healing in self, community, and globally*
Or others,	
Or in the world around you	
What touched you yesterday?	*Kinesthetic Healing Resources*
What did you allow to move you?	
What new perspectives,	*Audio/Digital Healing Resources*

What new ideas
Can you at this moment recall,
Easily.
Let them come to you as they will.　　　　　　　　　　　　*Permissive*
The deeper mind is thinking hundreds,　　　　　　　　　　*Strategy*
Thousands of times more
Than you are at the conscious level.

EMPOWERING THE INNER HEALER

Allow yourself to settle back where you are.	*Permission to be comfortable*
Allowing yourself to be present in this moment.	*Begin creating Mindfulness*
Tune into your breathing	*Notice how the following suggestions of breath, delivers its own sense of rhythmic breath; a rocking, inhaling, exhaling, pendulum-like rhythm*
Feel the parts of your breathing.	*One must first become aware that there are many different parts involved in breath; Listener shifts focus of attention to all the different parts involved in process of breathing. Following suggestions continue this ebb and flow effect...*
The air breathes in for you,	*Implying this is a natural automatic spontaneous process*
Then there's the letting go.	*Again, pacing the Listener's breath*
And then there's that little pause	
After you've breathed out	
And before the next breath comes in	
Let yourself sink deeply into that pause...	*Watch Listener's breath to coordinate with your words*
It's the quietest time of all	
For all your mind and body.	*When is there quiet time during the day?*
Feel the letting go	*The simplicity of breath assists in detachment*
With each breath out	
And with each letting go,	*On the out-breath, Listener releases stressors along with toxins and carbon monoxide*
Imagine your entire body is releasing	
All stress, all tension, releasing	
With each breath in	
You feel the coolness of the air	*Temperature awareness prepares Listener for nasal breathing suggestions:*
As it enters your nostrils.	
With each breath out	

Feel the warmth

And imagine with each breath out,Out-breath releases toxins, right?
You're breathing out

All unnecessary thoughts
Emptying your mind.Step out of Conscious Critical thoughts

And as your body growsClassically, the more your body relaxes,
the more your mind relaxes
More and more relaxed,
As your mind grow more and more relaxed
The emotions grow more and more open
Here in this safe place.Always a good idea to include safety
And as you sink into that pauseCareful; pause is 5 seconds, tops

Feel the little spark of energyRedirected attention to image of spark
That starts each breath inEnergy spark is automatic to breath
And think of that little spark of energyComparing energy to life
As a spark of life within you
And notice how ever deeply you relax
No matter how deeply and quietly relax
You slip into this pauseListener has done it before and is
accustomed to slipping into that long pause
No matter how *long* that pause becomes,Time Distortion;
Long / Little
And this *little* pauseAgain, cycle pace of delivery to Listeners' breath
Becomes this little spark of energy
Igniting the next breath.
And let this represent the desire of your Being
To be hereMindfulness
To live, Life renewing itselfPurpose of Life is to renew and heal
Again and again
With each breath.
And each breath breathes in oxygen.
And you can imagine breathing in

Pure White Light

White Light is supposedly known to be a healing force of color energy or allow the Listener to choose any color they wish to represent a color of their own

That flows in through your nostrils,
Flows through your nostrils
And swirls through your mind,
Swirls through your mind
And then flows down

*Flowing and
swirling and
swirling and
flowing*

Through all the rest of your body
Filling it with life and energy

Breath + Spark energy = Healing:

That little spark
Starts each new breath,
Each new breath fills you with healing.

Metaphor for Life Energy

Breathing creates Healing

And allow yourself to travel in your mind

*Permissive form of direct suggestion to mind-travel
In any way that works for you
Keeps Listener in control:
client centered*

To a sense of what is
Of heart and meaning for you.

Personalized Metaphor

What has deep spiritual value?

Remember, at this point the subconscious awareness is answering the questions that might seem difficult to answer at a conscious level

What touches you at a deep level?
It may be something that
You've traveled to in the past
It may be something that
You traveled to
Right here
In the moment.
Or perhaps you just allow
Your deeper mind

Creating Spiritual Resources

To take you
To a place,
Where you know what is of value to you;
What has spirit?
What nurtures your soul?

EMPOWERING HEALING RESOURCES

Create small motor catalepsy before you begin the following process:

When your eyelid muscles relax to the point	
Where they just don't want to open,	
And as you have that feeling	
Of relaxation in your eyelids,	
And as you very gently test them	
And as you test them,	*Inducing Hypnosis:*
	Bypassing Critical Factor
And as you test them let this relaxation	
Flow down through your body	*A flow of relaxation sounds like a little trickling brook, in a shady forest*
And as you test them again	*Convincer*
Even more gently	
Allow even more relaxation	*Comparison of "even more"*
And a more subtle feeling of relaxation to	*Deepening Technique*
Flow through all the muscles of your face,	
Your jaw, your neck and shoulders,	
Your arms and hands	*Progressive Relaxation, Body Scan*
Down to your fingertips	
As it reaches your fingertips	
Take a deep breath in	*Listener prone to comply with direction*
Draw it up to the center of your chest	
And as you feel your chest relax,	
Let yourself sink deeply into that *pause*	*Healing State*
After you breathe out	
And before the next breath comes in.	
And feel your chest and your abdomen relax,	*The body relaxes during the "Pause"*
Let it flow down through your pelvis	*Moving Relaxation Awareness "down" the body*
And your thighs	
And your knees	
And your legs and your feet.	

All the way down to the very tips of your toes.

And at anytime any unnecessary
Thoughts come along
You may erase those unnecessary

Thoughts from your mind.   *Preparing Subconscious*
for another "erase" image
about to be suggested again: repetition

This is your signal, it belongs to you   *Client-Centered Trance Logic*:
And you have the right
And the power to let go of any thoughts
That are not serving you
Unnecessary thoughts
Release them, erase them   *"Erasing" can create amnesia to*
the Subconscious mind

From your mental blackboard ;   *Easy imagery for almost*
everyone to relate to

As you gently test your eyelids,   *Convincer*
Imagine a wet *eraser*   *Eraser becomes metaphor*
vehicle for Mental Relaxation Suggestions

Going across the blackboard
Erasing any unnecessary mental thought.

And send another wave of relaxation through your body.   *"Wave" is another*
Water metaphor,
compounding image of "wet"

Good.
    Positive supportive Feedback

And if that same thought
Or any other thought comes along,
That's unnecessary
Just erase it.   *Now listener has the tool to erase*
thoughts that serve no purpose

Unnecessary thoughts
Or thoughts about the past or the future,
Questions, doubts, comparisons,

Judgments, criticisms,	
Unneeded right now.	
Allow yourself just to be here.	*Permission to create*
	Mindfulness in the Present Moment
Experience the stillness	*"Be still and know that I am God"*
As you sink deeply into that *pause*	*That place of quiet before igniting*
	the spark of healing through breath
After you breathe out	
And before you breathe in	*Process Imagery:*
	Coming into the Present Moment
The quietest time of all for your mind and body.	
And as you touch this place within	*Touching within implies*
	audio digital logic, Kinesthetic/Emotional
Allow yourself to just flow	*Permissive style*
Through time and space	
A little ways	*Time Travel*
To a time in that past	*Accessing Reference Memory:*
	Time, Inspiration, Love
That represents inspiration to you.	
A time perhaps when you felt	
Love and being loved.	*The most powerful of all human*
	emotional states
Maybe a time when you felt	
In deep communication	
With that Spirit	*Soon refers to spirit as Essence*
That moves though all things.	*Defining Moments of Epiphany*
A sacred moment,	
A holy moment,	
A moment of revelation, an epiphany,	
Or just a time of just feeling secure,	
Whole.	*Complete*
That time when the *Essence* of you	
Felt most at peace or most empowered;	*Drawing from Resource States*
And see what recollection comes to you	

It could be something from just a little while ago,	*Distorting Time Line*
Minutes or hours ago	
Days weeks or years;	
It could be something from your childhood.	*Utilizing Regressive State*
Let yourself float to that place	*Consistent use of floating Imagery*
As if you are riding on a magic carpet.	*"As If" engages imagination*
And bring it to mind	
Either *picture* it in your mind	*Using all sensory awareness:*
Or *hear* the sounds	
Feel yourself *touching* that experience within you	
*See, feel, touch, hear smel*l, but most of all,	
Let yourself *feel* the *sense* of Empowerment,	
Of Wholeness, of a Connection,	
A connection.	*Accessing Spiritual Resources*
And if that same thought or	
Any other thought comes along that's unnecessary	
Just erase it.	*Repetition / Erase*
Unnecessary thoughts	
Or thoughts about the past or the future,	*Grounding in this moment*
Questions, doubts, comparisons,	
Judgments, criticisms,	
Unneeded right now.	
Allow yourself just to be here.	*Mindfulness*
Experience the stillness	
As you sink deeply into that *pause*	*Repetition & Reinforcement*
After you breathe out	
And before you breathe in	
And know that you've gained	
And perhaps you can already begin to imagine	*Begin Future Pacing*
Some ways of using these aware nesses,	
These skills,	
In your own life,	

In your own healing	
And perhaps you can picture that.	*Subconscious image creates goal success*
Or think about it	
With something greater than just yourself,	*Spiritual Resource*
And allow yourself to feel the reality of that	*Permission to emote healing as a real experience*
And to notice where you feel it in your body	*Physical location of healing*
Maybe you feel it a little bit	*Comparison trance logic creates a Double Bind implies healing is experienced*
Or, maybe you feel it strongly.	
Breathe into that place within you	*Again, breathing into that place of healing within*
Where you feel that feeling	*Breathing into the feeling*
And as you breathe into it	
Let it grow stronger	
And let it spill out to every other cell of your body.	*Process Imagery*
Maybe it is a sense of knowing	*Intensifying and generalizing Awareness*
That there are possibilities with in you.	*Unlimited Potential*
And that you have a purpose for being here.	*Purposes of Healing*
And that purpose	
Has something to do with healing in some way.	
And imagine that you can trust	*Indirect Suggestion; Metaphor*
That this deeper place within you	
And the sense of *connection*	*Spiritual Resource*
That something that something is greater than you,	
A sense or *connection* with people,	
Or however it might form itself for you…	*Client Centered Image of Connection*
Imagine that you can allow this place within you	*Indirect Future Pacing*
This quality,	
This feeling	

This sense,	
To guide you.	*Listener learning to trust own self-healing abilities*
And as you *reflect* back	*Inner Digital Thought Process*
On the things that moved you today,	*Kinesthetic Thought Processing*
The things you touched upon	*Touched: Kinesthetic Suggestion*
Imagine that that deeper sense of Spirit	
Or Empowerment or Essence	
Can empower you to use those experiences	*Repetition: Empower*
To heal yourself	*Bottom Line:*
	We Can Heal Ourselves!
And those that you serve.	*As we facilitate healing in others*
Reflect back over the day	*By-pass word used as a*
	Direct Suggestion;
	Future Pacing
	Know that these gains are forever
And know that you've gained.	*Listener fills in their own benefits to this experience of hypnotic state*
And perhaps you can already begin	*Permissive language style*
To imagine some ways	
Of using these aware-nesses,	
These skills, in your own life,	
In your own healing	
And perhaps	
You can picture that.	
Or think about it.	*Bridging thought and the picture of health*

INNER CONNECTEDNESS

Note here how the Listener issue is feeling scared. Dr Miller's Reframe comes through the use of the keyword, Courage.

What do you say about the possibility	
Of really going into a relaxed state	
So that you can be in touch with yourself?	*Pretalk Suggestion*

Be in touch with yourself — *Process Goal Suggestion*
And be aware of the rather huge
Resources you have available
And then gaining access to your (courage)
So you can be free
To do the thing that you most want to do.
Is that o.k.? — *Verbal Contract of Agreement*

Begin by looking at my finger
And as you watch my finger, — *Instant Fixation of Attention*
Let your head remain where it is
And let your eyes follow up. — *Eye Roll Technique fatigues eye*
And as you continue to look at my finger — *Focusing Attention*
Slowly let your eyelids close by relaxing them.
Good. Great. — *Reinforcement, Reassurance*

Continue looking gently up — *Eyelids are closed at this time;*
On the back of your forehead — *Eyes turned upward behind closed eyes induces instant trance*

And imagine that there — *Imagination bridges mind to body*
On the back of the forehead,
You can see the word (i.e.: *courage*).
Or if there is some other symbol
That means (*courage*) to you
Visualize it. — *Visual cues represent courage*
Some people might see a lion — *Creating anchor*
As representing courage,
Or a certain hero or heroine,

Some symbol or something from (their own life)	
That represents courage for you.	
Visualize it, visualize it there	*Eyes are rolled upward*
On the back of your forehead	*inducing Alpha State*
As you do that	*Tasking the listener to relax*
Gradually allow your body to relax.	*by focusing on breath*
Tune into your breathing.	
Growing more and more comfortable with each breath.	
Take another deep breath in as you let it out,	*Listener follows direction*
Again picturing that symbol of ( )	*Keep symbol image consistent*
There on the back of your forehead	*Visual Reinforcement of Goal*
Allow your eyelid muscles to relax,	*paired with Healing Relaxation*
Down to the point they don't want to open.	*Small muscle catalepsy*
	proves Listener in compliance
And as you gently test them	*Make sure eyes stay closed allowing*
Let that relaxation	*progressive relaxation down the body*
Flow through the rest of your body	
The muscles of your face, your neck and shoulders,	*Body Scan*
Going down through your arms,	
Your wrists and your hands	
Down to your fingers.	
When you feel that relaxation in your fingertips	*Creating Assumption*
Take a deep breath in	
Draw it up through	
The arms and through the center of the chest	
And then releasing completely,	
Letting the air do the breathing for you.	*Surrendering to the*
	Wisdom of the body
Growing more and more relaxed	
More comfortable with each breath.	*Compounding of Relaxation*
Each breath relaxing your abdomen,	*Continuing down the body*
Relaxation flowing all the way down	*Repetition of Relaxation*
Through your abdomen	
Your pelvis, and thighs, knees and ankles	

All the way down to the tips of your toes
Releasing completely.

Good.

Any time any unnecessary thoughts come along,   *Direct Suggestion*
                                                                                          Mental Relaxation Technique

Just erase those unnecessary thoughts
From your mind
Because they are not needed.

Allowing yourself to be present, good.   *Mindfulness*

And as you relax,
Remember for a moment,   *Regress to past relaxation memory*
The things that you've experienced
Within the last months and years,
In particular,
Remember how valuable it has been for you to relax,   *Resource*
And how you can begin to move in the right direction…….

And to know that you're able to do this
By letting go of all unnecessary thoughts
By trusting yourself,
And by having confidence in who you are   *Letting go*
                                                                             unnecessary thoughts =
                                                      Not considering options that
                                     listener has decided will not work
By having confidence in who you are
And in your higher power.   *Triggering Spiritual Anchor*

And let yourself be in contact with that part of you   *Kinesthetic Accessing*
Let yourself be in contact
With that part of you that has grown during this time.   *Assumes Success*

And as you feel the contact with that part of yourself,
Let your finger move to let me know *Listener is Aphasic*
so it's hard to speak
That you can feel it. *Developing non-verbal signal*
through Ideomotor response;

Good.

This is the Inner part of you, *Connecting to Spirit*
A part of you always there,
Always there, always willing to serve you.
Creating Self-Trust.
And on many occasions in the past *Reflecting on Past*
to be more Present

Has it allowed you to achieve things
That were difficult.
And go back to another time *Availability and richness of recall*
When you were able to use
Your higher power with (i.e.: *other relationships*.)

That was in you
To change what you wanted to change.
And in your mind, just re-live that experience, *Accessing spiritual*
resource through Revivication

To discover the power.
Remember it,
And know that it is real
As you continue to erase any distractions. *Releasing unhelpful thoughts*
Let your YES finger move
When you feel that quality of empowerment *Ideomotor Signal*
convinces Listener it is real

And along with it allow yourself
To really be in touch with *Relating touch as an ideomotor signal*
The potential for the Higher Power *Reminder of Potential*
To serve and work through you.

And all those things that you have *seen*	
That are possible with this Higher Power	
And the *gratitude* that you have had for	*Accessing Gratitude Resource*
What it has allowed you to accomplish,	
Keep all this awareness with you	
As you let go of these thoughts of the past.	*In with the Good, out with the Bad*
Let yourself look forward in the future,	*Future Pacing to Write one's own script*
A little while ago we talked about	
(making a decision, expressing self more,	
following through on it, etc).	
Be in touch with this need and strength within	*Connection through touch*
And visualize yourself,	*Future Imaging of what must be done to create Listener success*
One by one	*Break down task into simple steps*
Taking the steps you need to take,	
And let your voice tell me what you need to do.	*Seeking Verbal Feedback*
What's the first step?	*Allow Listener to respond*
Visualize that happening.	*Create visual picture of the action*
When you feel that you	*Connecting image to ability to act*
Now you can do it	
And feel yourself doing it,	
Can do it,	
Let your yes finger move.	*Non-Verbal ideomotor response from Subconscious*
Good.	

Having done that, allow yourself to relax, Feeling yourself be able to do that	*Associating this relaxation* *to creating resources* *necessary* *for success*
Having (- *state listener resource* -) And for your self Your higher power, And truth and integrity Visualize yourself doing that, However it comes to you now.	*Give Listener a moment to imagine*
Tell me what the next step is.	*Allow Listener time to verbalize*

PROCESSING RESOURCES

And as you return to this moment,
Still in touch with of those feelings.
(i.e.: the Courage, the Confidence, the Clarity)
The willingness to know,
To do what you know is right
In spite of what other things
May be pulling on you.
Doing what you needed to do,
Doing what you knew was right in spite of…others.
And for your self
Your Higher Power,
And Truth and Integrity   *Calling forward Resources*
Visualize yourself doing that However it
comes to you now.

Tell me what the next step is.   *Seeking verbal feedback*

Visualize the next step. However it comes to you.

What do you do after that?

What's the next step after that?   *Continuing to create Outcome*
                                                     or Successful Out-picture
Picture it happening, however it comes to you.
As you see it happen,
Feel it happen.   *Synthesia:Connects seeing,feeling*
Good.

What's the next step after that?   *Logically following steps to success*
Again, picture that happening.   *Intensifies Positive Outcome*
Centered, calm.
And what do you see after that?   *Creating sequence to action*
Vision yourself free,
Independent,
Fully in touch with your deeper needs.   *Reinforce*
Feeling REALLY confident in yourself,   *Keyword "Confidence"*

Knowing that the time has come	*No better time than NOW*
To honor that Truth of who you are,	*That part of Listener*
	that must be trusted
Down in your heart,	*Opening Portals of Self-Trust*
Your willingness to *love*,	*One of the powerful forces*
	in the Universe
To be close,	
To develop real intimate relationships;	*Outcome: Ideal image*
The willingness to be honest with your body	*Outcome Ideal for Body*
And what it needs,	
What it needs	
To be nurtured with;	*Safety Images-/nurturing, protection*
And also what it needs	
To be protected from.	
Willing to honor your mind	*Outcome ideal for Mind*:
Your ability to think	*Self Trust*
And to choose wisely	
Based on your truth,	
Letting go of all the ways	*Detaching from old ways*
	of decision-making
You may have made	
Decisions in the past.	*That was then, and this is NOW*
Protecting your body.	
Calming your emotions.	*Pacing & Reinforcement*
Connecting with those people	*of Connection*
That are really important to you.	
Gaining the support of those connections	
Realizing more than ever	
That you are connected.	*(Whether we like it or not!)*

APPENDIX

IMAGINATION EXERCISES

If you are looking to test your listener's Imagination Quotient, the following exercises are great to learn and use. Notice the italicized words to encourage imagination in the participant. Formally known as Imagination Tests, we have dropped that concept as one may not pass a test, right?

FIRST CHALLENGE: BOOK AND BALLOONS

And now,
Extend your arms and hands straight in front of you
As though your hands were on a table in front of you
And while you're holding your hands out
Imagine that someone is placing a brick
On the back of your right hand.
Just *visualize* a brick being placed on the
Back of your right hand.

Feel the coarseness of the underside of the brick
Feel its weight
Imagine can see its dark red color
Feel its weight,
Its heaviness.

And then, *imagine* someone is coming along with a helium filled balloon
A ribbon tied around the neck of that balloon and the
Other end of that ribbon tied around
The wrist of the left hand
So that the helium filled balloon is
Pulling upward
Feel that pressure,
Upward from below.

And then, *see* the brick on top of your right hand
And *imaging* that a sand bag is being placed
On top of the brick on the back of your right hand
And *feel* the increased weight
Pressing down.

The Heart of Hypnosis & Deep Healing Workbook

And tie another helium filled balloon around the wrist of your left hand,
And you have a red balloon
And a green balloon floating
Up toward the ceiling.

And now *imagine* someone comes along
And puts a chain on top of the brick.
And pressing down heavily
On the back of your right hand.

And tie another balloon,
A yellow balloon around the wrist of your left hand,
And *just notice* the *difference in the feeling* between the two hands.

Notice *which one feels* light or heavy.
And then open your eyes
And *see if you notice* a difference
Between the height of the two hands.

(And then let the hands rest on your lap or the table in front of you)

SECOND IMAGINATION CHALLENGE:

Now,
Clasp your two fingers like this,
Extend your two index fingers
Rightly clasped
Just the two index fingers extended.
And make a space of about
½ inch space between them.
Pull them apart so there is a space.
Now, *focus on that space between the two fingers*
And *imagine* your two fingers
Are like two powerful magnets   *Comparisons are powerful metaphors*
Pulling toward each other.
Feel the force pulling the fingers closed,
Closer and closer
No matter how hard you pull them apart
Feel the force pulling them closed.
Watch the space.
And pulling them together
Watch the space getting smaller and smaller
Feel a force pull them closed…
Feel the space smaller and smaller
And the magnets pulling them together.
Feel the magnets getting stronger,
Feel the magnets getting stronger and stronger.

This open-eyed hypnosis experience works almost all the time and is a great convincer to the participant of ability to focus and concentrate on a task. Additionally, as it heightens the imagination, it is a great pre-curser to the formal hypnotic experience.

The repetition of the word FEEL becomes very important here to a successful completion of the task, as it teaches us that what we FEEL creates our reality. If we FEEL poorly, we perform poorly. If we FEEL energetic and alive, we are more likely to BE more energetic and alive!

THIRD IMAGINATION CHALLENGE:

Now,
Rest your hands again.

Clasp them again really tight
And squeeze your hands
Like you're squeezing a lemon.

And as you squeeze,
Concentrate on the feeling
That super glue is oozing
Is oozing out of the pores of your hands and fingers,
And beginning to glue the hands tightly together.

It takes a moment to know it has been set
A certain moment you know it has been set,
Doesn't feel so wet anymore,
But feels solid.
When you *try* to pull your hands apart,   *TRY connotes failure to Subconscious Mind*

And notice how tightly stuck together they are.
Feel how tight that glue sticks.

Try to pull them apart.

See if you can pull hard enough to get them apart.

And then immerse those hands in a warm solvent   *Utilizing imagination to come out of the trance state*

It is melting the glue,
And notice as you feel the glue dissolve
And as it does you notice how easily
They come apart.   *(Model pulling your hands apart for the client)*

And you can pull your hands apart...
They stick a little bit but
And you can get them apart now.

ENGAGING IMAGINATION

Law of Concentrated Attention (DEMONSTRATION)

Here's a great little script to use with client when you want to concentrate and narrow their attention to a particular mental representation. In this case, it's the old classic Lemon Demo. Listener will experience psychological and behavioral changes that tend to occur which are consistent with the prompted word/image held in memory, and salivation usually occurs.

Close your eyes and *imagine*
That you have a lemon.
Imagine you are *holding* the lemon in your hand.
Imagine the *color*.
Imagine you can *feel the smooth*
Yet *bumpy surface* of the lemon.
Now, is that lemon *round* like a ball
Or does it *come to a point?*
Feel the firmness of the lemon.
Drop it on the table
And *hear the sound* it makes
When it *hits the kitchen table*.
Now take out a very *sharp* knife
Cut it and
Look at the cut surface of the lemon,
You can even *see the seeds cut*,
That's how *sharp* the knife is.
Bring that lemon close to your *nose*
So you can *smell* its fragrance
And then *open* your *mouth* and
Sink your teeth
Into the *sour* lemon and
Suck the juice into your mouth.
Let the *juice flow over your tongue*.
Feel it and *notice* what happens in your mouth.

Imagery is the creation of a multi-sensory representation of an event or entity not actually present. To the Deeper Mind, Imagery is the same whether it is triggered by events outside or inside the nervous system.

PUTTING IT ALL TOGETHER:
INDUCTION / SUGGESTION / EMERGENCE

Let yourself become aware that in this moment in time	*Leading listener / Permissive Instruction Fixating attention*
That there is no other place	
That you need to go.	*Beginning detachment*
That there's not anything else you need to do;	*to compound off this suggestion*
	De-Tasking:
No problem that you have to solve,	
There's nothing you have to accomplish,	
There's nothing you need to figure out.	
Everything outside of this room	*Continue detachment by stepping out of this galaxy!*
Can be a million miles away.	*Heightened awareness of Inner Experience; diminished awareness of outer world*
The entire universe could get along without you	
For the next few minutes.	*Time distortion*
Be aware of that,	*Be aware that time has been distorted*
Be aware that this is fundamentally true	*The Subconscious loves to hear The TRUTH*
Whether you are aware of it or not,	*Confusion technique with double bind*
And be aware of it.	*Direct / Paternal Suggestion*
As much as possible, observing	*Creating safety with built in sense of possibility*
Without doing anything,	*Reinforcement of detachment*
Let your eyes look upward	*"Take over" by hypnotist with specific suggestions*
Until you are looking upward toward the ceiling.	

And without moving your head back	*This upward strain begins to*
Just look upward toward the ceiling.	*fatigue the eye muscles*
While you are looking up	*Following action creates an immediate Alpha brainwave state:*
Slowly let your eyelids close	
While you're still looking upward	
Toward the back of your forehead.	
Imagine you can see the word relax	*Creating an inner hallucination*
On the back of your forehead	*re-directing specific location*
As long as you keep your eyes rolled up	*If / then logic:*
	Cause & Effect
Looking up at the back of your forehead,	*Creating eye fatigue w/ fixation*
It causes the muscles of your eyelids to relax.	*for desired effect*
If you keep your eyes looking up and	*Implied if / then logic*
Gently try to open your eyelids	*TRY connotes subconscious failure*
And <u>see</u> if you can <u>feel</u> their relaxation.	*Mixed; Visual/Kinesthetic*
Let that relaxation stay in your eyelids	*Implying that there is relaxation*
Test them a little bit harder	*Direct suggestion as a convincer;*
Let the relaxation stay	*immediate reinforcement of relaxation*
That's because when you do this	*Trance logic begins*
You bring into play	
A certain reflex that relaxes the eyelid muscles.	*Expert/Prestige*
And imagine,	*By-pass word*
As long as you keep your eyes looking up,	*Imagination engaged*
As you test your eyelids	*Convincer keeps listener's control*
You can let the relaxation you have in your eyelids,	*Permission, assumes relaxation*
Flow throughout the rest of your body.	
Let that relaxation flow through the rest of your body	*Kinesthetic reinforcement of relaxation and nonlocal relaxation through body*
And gently <u>try</u> to open up your eyelids.	*Direct Suggestion to fail*
Let it stay in your eyelids, and	*Permissive Suggestion*
Test them a little bit harder.	*Reinforcement of Convincer*

Imagine as you test your eyelids,	*Engaging and Bridging*
	to Subconscious thru Imagination
Let that relaxation flow through the	*Selective Awareness*
Rest of your body.	*Reinforcement of physical release*
While you are looking up	*Following action creates an immediate*
	Alpha brainwave state:
Slowly let your eyelids close	
While you're still looking upward	
Toward the back of your forehead.	
Imagine you can see the word RELAX	*Creating an inner hallucination*
On the back of your forehead.	*re-directing specific location*
As long as you keep your eyes rolled up	*If / then logic:*
	Cause & Effect
Looking up at the back of your forehead,	*Creating eye fatigue w/ fixation*
It causes the muscles of your eyelids to relax.	*for desired effect*
If you keep your eyes looking up and	*Implied if / then logic*
Gently try to open your eyelids	*TRY connotes subconscious failure*
And <u>see</u> if you can <u>feel</u> their relaxation	
	Mixed; Visual/Kinesthetic
Let that relaxation stay in your eyelids	*Implying that there <u>is</u> relaxation*
Test them a little bit harder	*Direct suggestion as a Convincer*
Let the relaxation stay	*w/ immediate relaxation reinforcement*
That's because when you do this	*Trance logic begins*
You bring into play	
A certain reflex that relaxes the eyelid muscles.	*Expert/Prestige*
And imagine,	*By-pass word*
As long as you keep your eyes looking up,	*Imagination engaged*
As you test your eyelids	*Safety: Convincer keeps client in control*
You can let the relaxation you have in your eyelids,	*Permission*
	assumes relaxation
Flow throughout the rest of your body.	
Let that relaxation flow through the rest of your body	*Kinesthetic*
	reinforcement of relaxation and
	nonlocal relaxation through body
And gently <u>try</u> to open up your eyelids.	*Direct Suggestion to fail*

Let it stay in your eyelids, and	Permissive Suggestion
Test them a little bit harder.	Reinforcement of Convincer
Imagine as you test your eyelids,	Engaging and Bridging to Subconscious thru Imagination
Let that relaxation flow through the	Selective Awareness
Rest of your body.	Reinforcement of physical release
Imagine as you test your eyelids	Imagination engaged locally
Let that relaxation flow through	
The rest of your body.	Reinforcement
Imagine ripples flowing outward like a	Imagery engaged with
Stone thrown into the quiet surface of a still pond.	soothing image
Imagine those ripples flowing out through your forehead	Mental/physical blend of imagery
Throughout all the muscles of your face,	Begin Body Scan, or progressive relaxation
Feel the weight of your lower jaw	Light trance physical awareness
As your upper and lower teeth gently separate.	Action releases mandible tension
Many people clench their teeth.	Identification with others / (Milton Erickson)
That's a place that tension is held	Location of tension identified
As the jaw gently droops open	Mandible release
And you may even feel your teeth part	Sensory Awareness / Convincer
And you are letting that tension go.	AND = Cause & Effect; Release
Let that relaxation flow down	Permissive Suggestion
Into your neck,	moving downward
And into your shoulders	
And down through your arms,	DOWN
Elbows, forearms, wrists and your hands	
All the way down to your fingers	DOWN Reinforced
And notice what it feels like when it	Feeling Awareness
Reaches the tips of your fingers	
A feeling of letting go;	FEELING
Maybe a tingling or a warmth or a pulsation	FEELING
When you feel that feeling in your fingertips	FEELING
Take a deep breath in	

And draw that relaxation from your fingertips	
Up into the center of your chest	UP
And as you let that breath out,	Exhale
Let it be a feeling of letting go.	
And then just let the air do the breathing for you.	Turning over to Higher Power within
Let the rising and the falling of your chest	Centers focus in chest
Be a soothing feeling of peace	Feeling = Soothing
Like the rising and falling of swells on the ocean.	(Metaphor paced to client breath)
And let that relaxation flow through your	
Chest and your abdomen	Comparing body to ocean
Through your upper back and your lower back.	
Let the rising and falling	continued pacing of client breath in and out (down and up)
Of your abdomen be like a gentle massage	
To all your internal organs	
And let the relaxation	Allowing / Permissive
Flow down into the pelvis	Relaxation moving downward
Relaxing all the pelvic organs that are	
Flowing into your thighs and your knees	
Down to your legs and ankles	
And down to your feet	Continues downward
And all the way to the tips of your toes,	
Just letting go.	Detachment / Reinforcement
Because you know in your mind,	Trance Logic of belief to Detach
That there's no where you need to go	
And nothing that has to be done	
Then you can allow the muscles of your body	
To release and relax and do nothing.	
Good.	
Remember, the relaxation is already there	Reinforcement
And all you need to do is	

Let go of the tension to discover it…	*End of Trance Induction*
	Pregnant Pause engages Depth
	Imagination / Bridge to Subconscious
Now let yourself take a little journey	*Tasking Safety:*
In your imagination	*Bridging mind/body message*
Imagine drifting off to a place	
That is very pleasant,	*Suggestion of Safety*
Some place far away from anything	*All-inclusive*
That could ever disturb you.	
A place of peace and calm.	*Implied relaxation suggestion*
Maybe a place you have been in the past	*Regressive / Resource*
That has been very pleasant for you.	*Guided Imagery begins*
Could be a tropical island,	
Or a beautiful mountain,	
You could be skiing or swimming	
Or just sitting back on a deck chair,	
Or taking a walk through a beautiful place.	
Whatever season of the year	
You would like it to be	
Go there.	*Takeover w/ Direct Suggestion*
Picture it in your mind as clearly as you can	*Internal Hallucination*
Perhaps you can let yourself see the colors,	
The shapes,	
The movement around you.	*Movement=Energy*
And hear the sounds.	*External Audile Hallucination*
Smell the fragrances in the air,	*External Olfactory Hallucination*
Feel the textures that touch your body	*Sensory Awareness*
Little breezes of air.	
And anytime	*Reinforcing Safety*
Any unnecessary thoughts come along	
Just let them go.	*Reinforcement of Detachment*
Just release them and refocus	
On this beautiful place	
Of serenity and peace and calm and safety.	
Good.	*Listener assumes accomplished task*

And as you enjoy this peaceful place	Assumption creates enjoyment
Be aware that having visited here	Begin Post Hypnotic
And having allowed yourself to relax this time	
You may do so again anytime that you wish	Post Hypnotic Suggestion
And only when you wish.	Tasking; keeps client in control
All you need to do is think about this place	PHS Reinforcement to relax
And give yourself permission	
To let go.	Detachment/ Deepening
Knowing that there's no other place that you need to be	
And nothing else that you need to do.	Permission to relax
And in a matter of seconds,	Expectancy through Future Pacing
You feel yourself relaxing,	Kinesthetic
Visualizing this place in your mind.	Visual
Each time, you relax,	
Not only will it be more rapid if you wish	Dr. Flowers Concept
But you can also relax to an even deeper level.	Implication of Levels
And soon you'll find that being relaxed is a	
Very natural thing to do.	Natural = Safety
And you'll find many uses for this relaxation	Subconscious works on many different levels
Remembering that only you can initiate	Responsibility and ability
The process of relaxation.	
Others can participate only with your permission.	Keeps client in control
This is your mind, it belongs to you.	Yes Set begins
This is your body, it belongs to you.	Yes Set continues
And when you relax in this way	Trance logic creates third Yes Set
It allows you to accept those things that you wish to accept,	Permission to change
Will allow you to act with more commitment and power	
To change the things that you really want to change.	
It will allow you to accept with serenity those things	Serenity= acceptance
That you know it is wise to accept.	Internal Resource of wisdom
And the inner experiences	

That you have when you relax	
Will lead you to ever deeper levels	*Deepening*
Of understanding and wisdom	*Reinforcement of Internal Resource*
Concerning yourself,	
The world around you.	
And take you to a place of true peace,	
Love and freedom, if you wish.	*3 Powerful energies for change;*
	Permissive-client centered
Now, visualize in your minds' eye	*Evoking imagination as a*
	bridge to body
Yourself looking and feeling completely well and healthy.	*Future Pace*
Imagine you can look ahead	
A few weeks or months into the future.	
Imagine your body in really, in vibrant good health,	*Locking image into*
	Subconscious
Full of vim and vigor.	*Kinesthetic Suggestion*
The muscles of your body,	*Visual Suggestion*
Strong and vigorous.	*Kinesthetic Suggestion*
Your body weighing just what you want it to weigh.	*Personally, I'd rather use the image of ideal shape and body form rather than "weight" as I doubt if Subconscious can image weight as a "pound" or a kilo" or an "ounce", etc.*
Moving the way you want it to move.	*Kinesthetic Hallucination*
Again, you can stay in your special place	*Double Bind Permission*
	to feel emotions
Or you can go to any other place you can	*You can do this,*
	or you can do that
For you to feel all of your emotions,	
Imagine your healthy body and your healthy emotions.	*Imagination*
	bridging body/mind
Imagine you can use them with the power you want	*Power=empowerment*
To empower yourself	
To do the things you want to do.	

Your mind is clear,	*Sets the resolve to change*
You can focus on what you want to focus on,	*then focuses on the change*
And release those things you want to release.	*Starting off with a clean slate*
Your relationships with others are positive.	*Addressing relationships*
You feel success and creativity	*Kinesthetic notion of success*
In all the things you are doing.	*ALL things / universal coverage*
A look of wisdom in your eyes,	*Visual Suggestion / implied sagacity*
Forehead at peace,	*Physical reference of peace awareness*
Your heart strong,	*Physical reference of strength*
Filled with calm energy	*Kinesthetic*
In touch with the	
Deepest essence of yourself	*Self-connection*
That you can be aware of.	*Reinforcement of Awareness*
Continuing to erase any other	
Thoughts that come along.	*Deepening*
Notice your experience at this moment	*Beginning Change / Trance logic*
And find the most positive aspect	*Tasking the listener*
Of this experience of this moment.	
And think of a word, or a phrase	
That can represent this most	
Positive aspect of this experience;	*Subconscious reviews experience; reinforces all ego-enhancing suggestions in the process*
Just let it come to you	*Permissive*
And think now,	*Who is being addressed, subconscious or self?*
Say it to yourself in your mind.	*Anchoring begins*
This will serve as an anchor, or a cue.	*Post hypnotic suggestion begins*
And anytime in the future,	*Future Posting anchor of Hypnotic experience*
If you would like to get back	
In touch with this experience,	*Simple Ideo-Sensory suggestion*

You may do so by	*Anchoring directions/ Tasking*
Relaxing yourself,	*#1*
Thinking this image,	*#2*
And repeating this word.	*#3*
And then you can return quickly back to this place.	*Posting suggestion for next time*

And if you're busy doing something else and even
If you're not able to stop
In the course of what you're doing,
If you simply just think this word,   *Think = internal anchor:*
You'll notice greater focus   *implied If / Then logic*
Greater centering
And ongoing deeper awareness

Of whom you are.   *Ego Enhancing Suggestion*
Good.

Now, gradually allow yourself to return	
Back to this place	*Begin Emerging*
Where you are seated in this room.	*Creating physical awareness*
Sense the positions of your body,	
Feel its relaxation	*Reinforcement of good feelings*
Be aware of the day	*External Awareness to dehypnotize*
Be aware of what you are doing here	
Almost as though you were taking a little nap,	*Returning back to wakefulness*
As if you were on a little journey.	*Metaphorically speaking*
And now you are returning back	
Gradually re-awakening.	*Gentle repetition of Return / Emerging*
Letting your body begin to stretch	
And move a little bit.	*Insures listener is following directions*
Coming all the way back,	*Giving listener time to respond*
Breathing a little more deeply	*Use breath to disconnect from trance*
Maybe stretching your neck and your head,	*Physical movement returns*
Your shoulders,	

Feet or your fingers
Come all the way back.
And when you're ready
Take a deep breath in and
As you let that breath out,
And your eyelids open   *Dehypnotization*
And just think to yourself   *PHS Self-talk Suggestion*
Wide awake and present   *Mindfulness*
Here and now.
Good.   *Assurance and Permission*
                 to Maintain Mindfulness

A LEXICON OF HYPNOTIC TERMS AND PHRASES

A

Abreaction: An action whereby emotionally charged material/feelings, etc. is released from the mind and psyche through reliving a past incident; bringing to consciousness that which was formerly unconscious or repressed. Mind and Body relives Initial Sensitizing Event

Absorption of Attention: Necessary for successful trance. The client's attention is focused on a spot on a ceiling, a story, a physical feeling. Eye fixation, eye closure, hypnotic mask, diminished movement are signs indicating absorption of attention.

Abstraction: Process of developing concepts; that is, grouping objects in terms of some distinguishing common property.

Acetylcholine: A neurotransmitter. In the brain it helps regulate memory. In the peripheral nervous system, controls the actions of skeletal and smooth muscle.

Action Potential: An electrical potential that occurs when a neuron is activated and temporarily reverses the electrical state of its interior membrane from negative to positive. This electrical charge travels along the axon to the neuron's terminal where it triggers or inhibits the release of a neurotransmitter.

Addiction: Development of physical or psychological dependence on a drug, event, or action that craving and physical/psychological discomfort or pain occurs in its absence.

Affect: A strong emotional feeling.

Affect Bridge: A technique by which significant memories are to be recovered by inducing a previous intense emotional state in a client and asking him or her to remember a past instance when he or she felt the same disturbing feelings to create a resource to resolve the problem.

Afferent Neuron: Neuron that carries messages toward the central nervous system from a receptor cell. Also known as a sensory neuron.

Age Progression: Simulated time orientation. The hypnotic subject hallucinates, living in the future while retaining his / her chronological age; also known as Future Pacing.

Age Regression: the phenomenon of returning in one's mind, as well as one's behavior to an earlier, subsequent period in one's life.

Alignment: To match another person's behavior or experience by getting into the same line of sight and thought as the person.

Altered State of Consciousness: Any non-ordinary mental states, including meditation, hypnosis, and drug induced states.

All-Or-Nothing Law: Principle that if a nerve fiber responds at all, it responds with full strength.

Alpha Rhythms: The electrical rhythm typical of the brain during normal wakefulness. About 8 to 12 oscillations per second; Hrz

Alpha State: A light to medium state of hypnosis which can be used inter actively with a client. Also associated with the dream state and REM.

Alternate Life Progression: The ability to project one's consciousness into a future time line.

Alternate Life Regression: The ability to return in ones imagination to an earlier time and place in another time line.

Ambiguity: Deliberately used ambiguous suggestions encouraging client's projections and meanings: One can be quite iron willed and hardheaded in such matters … (leaves it open to interpretation whether hypnotist is praising perseverance or criticizing stubbornness.)

Amnesia: An inability to recall past memories or experiences. Hypnotic amnesia can either happen spontaneously or be produced by suggestion. Loss of memory; it can be total or partial.

Amnesia: Posthypnotic: loss of memory for happenings occurring during hypnosis for whatever the hypnotist suggested to forget. Spontaneous: form of amnesia occurring in subject without receiving any suggestion   to this effect . Spontaneous amnesia is often a simple psychological defense mechanism.

Analgesia: The insensitivity to pain either locally or widespread. Can be brought on by suggestion. Absence of the sense of pain.

Anchor: An anchor is the action of tying in a new ending/response to an existing or constant stimulus. A specific stimulus: sight, sound, word or touch that automatically brings up a particular memory and state of body and mind. Example: "Our song."

And: A word that leads and links. Following a pacing statement "You feel the comfort of that one deep breath", then leads, "and" you can use that one deep breath to sink deeper and deeper.; cause and effect.

Anesthesia: The loss of all sensory modalities. An agent that causes insensitivity to pain.

Anima: In Carl Jung's theory, an archetype representing femaleness or the female principal within the psyche.

Animal Magnetism: Anton Mesmer's name for hypnotism based on his assumption that hypnosis is related to the state of ordinary magnetism; Mesmerism.

Animus: In Jung's theory, an archetype representing maleness or the male principal within the psyche.

Anxiety: A feeling of painful or apprehensive uneasiness closely related to fear, especially that is characterized by dread or anticipation of some unclear threat.

Apposition of Opposites: An example of hypnotic language, this techniques juxtaposes polarities or opposites: "as the right hand becomes light, your body can sink even deeper into heaviness and relaxation. . . Experiment with warm / cold, up / down, light / heavy, right / left, floats / sink, etc."

Aphasia: Disturbance in language comprehension or production.

Archetype: An original pattern, prototype, or idea on which others are modeled. In Jung's theory, universal

primordial images found in the collective unconscious.

Arm Catalepsy: A suspension of physical movement, an effective, rapid and highly directive means to trance induction.

Arm Levitation: A technique of raising a subject's arm by giving a suggestion of weightlessness.

Associated: Seeing the world out of your own eyes. Experiencing life in your body. Contrast with Dissociated.

Auditory Nerve: A bundle of nerve fibers extending from the cochlea of the ear to the brain, which contains two branches: the cochlear nerve that transmits sound information and the vestibular nerve that relays information related to balance.

Authoritarian: The approach of hypnotic suggestion that is commanding and forceful in nature. A suggestion that conveys it is being imposed by the hypnotist.

Auto(genic) Hypnosis: synonymous with Self-Hypnosis. A procedure where a person develops into a good subject, thoroughly trained in proper instruction allowed to be carried out by themselves.

Autonomic Nervous System (ANS): A branch of the peripheral nervous system concerned with involuntary functions of the body. That part of the nervous system that regulates bodily activities not ordinarily subject to voluntary control. Its activities are divided between the sympathetic and parasympathetic divisions.

Auditory Nerve: A bundle of nerve fibers extending from the cochlea of the ear to the brain, which contains two branches: the cochlear nerve that transmits sound information and the vestibular nerve that relays information related to balance.

Automatic Writing: The unconscious action of writing, performed in a state of trance.

Auto Rotary Movements: The impossibility to stop a rotary movement (generally of the forearms) once it has been started by the hypnotist.

Auto-Suggestion: Suggestions made to oneself through affirmations, obsessive thoughts, wishful thinking, etc; self-talk absorbed by the subconscious mind; the action of giving oneself suggestions.

Aversive Conditioning: Use of an unpleasant or painful stimulus to reinforce learning.

Avoidance: Refraining from anything that makes one feel bad.

Axon: The fiber like extension of a neuron by which the cell sends information to target cells.

Axiomatic: taken for granted; self evident as in Axiomatic signs of trance

B

Bardo State: A definition for the place where the soul goes in between incarnations; a place of rest and to review lessons learned in different lives.

Behavior: The activity of organisms.

Behavior Modification: Application of principles of learning to change or eliminate unwanted or abnormal behavior.

Belief: Trust or confidence that is learned or experienced from the past. Thought accepted as truth.

Beta State: Our most active mental state. You are most likely in beta right now!

Behavior: The activity of organisms. Rhythms in the EEG of a frequency of about 25 per second.

Bias: A strongly held personal opinion about someone or something; the judgment could be conscious or unconscious, favorable or unfavorable.

Bind of Comparable Alternatives: Used by Milton Erickson it gives client a choice between two or more alternatives offering the illusion of choice: Would you like to go into a light trance, or a medium trance or a deep trance today? Or, "what you hear may be used in your personal life, or perhaps in your career, or incorporate it into your life experiences.

Biofeedback: A technique allowing one to monitor and control his or her own internal bodily functions.

Bodily Image: The person's perception of self.

Body Image: A mental picture that describes the way you see your body.

Boundaries: The defense systems each person uses to protect his or her body, thoughts and feelings.

Brain: The central nervous system above the spinal cord.

Brainstem: The major route by which the forebrain sends information to and receives information from the spinal cord and peripheral nerves. It controls respiration and regulation of heart rhythms.

Break State: Diffusion technique used for clearing current thoughts Deepening technique.

Bridging: A technique that tells client, "as this happens, this will happen"; cause and effect link.

Broca's Area: Brain region located in frontal lobe of left hemisphere that is important speech production.

Bruxism: Grinding or gnashing of one's teeth, presents as unresolved stress in an unconscious state.

Burnout: Vague term used describing the physical and emotional exhaustion that accompanies stress.

Bypass Word: Words that by pass the critical mind to enter into subconscious more easily.

C

Catalepsy: A state of hyper suggestibility in which an individual will display signs of body rigidity that goes beyond their usual conscious state's ability. A state in which the subject has no external sensitivity and cannot perform voluntary movements. It is usually manifested by a rigidity of the body or certain parts of the body. In this condition the body and the limbs will keep any position in which they are placed; ratifies or proves the trance experience.

Cataleptic: A person who can go into and remain in the state of catalepsy.

Catharsis: The act of releasing stored charged emotions either of an uncomfortable or a pleasant nature.

Causality (Causal interpretation): Relation between cause and effect; correlated events or phenomena. i.e. "As you hear that hammer next door you imagine that it's driving you deeper and deeper relaxed." Sequence of events that mind connects from habit. If, then logic.

Central Nervous System (CNS): That portion of the nervous system that lies within the skull and spinal

column; the brain and spinal cord.

Cerebral Cortex: The part of the brain associated with conscious experience and higher mental processes. A grayish rind of tissue covering the cerebrum.

Cerebral Hemispheres: They are symmetrical halves of the brain. There are two occipital lobes, two parietal lobes and two frontal lobes. These two hemispheres are in continual communication with one other. Each functions as an independent parallel processor with complementary functions.

Cerebrum: The main part of the brain, divided into right and left hemispheres; known as the new brain.

Chiastic Structure: Gives meaning to boring repetitions and keeps listener interested: Old King Cole was a merry old soul and a merry old soul was he; 7 up, you like it, it likes you.

Chunk Size: The level of specificity: People who are detail orientated are "*small chunks.*" People who think in general terms are "*large chunks*" - they see the big picture.

Client Centered Therapy: A form of therapy designed by Carl Rogers in which the client assumes responsibility for solving own problems. The therapist's role is to clarify and assist, not to give advice.

Clinical Hypnosis: Hypnosis that is performed by a professional hypnotist under certain standard guidelines or conditions; therapeutic application of hypnosis.

Co-dependence: A pattern of painful dependence on compulsive behavior and a need for approval from others in an attempt to find safety, self-worth and identity.

Comfort Assessment Scale: A method reframing Pain Scale to focus on comfort rather than pain

Compounding: Build suggestions one on top of the other to create subconscious awareness and reinforcement.

Cortex: This is where most high-level functions associated with the mind are implemented. Some of its regions are highly specialized. For example, the motor cortex helps coordinate all voluntary muscle movements. The occipital lobes located near the rear of the brain interprets visual stimuli.

Confusion Technique: A delivery of unlinked ideas that quickly bypass Critical Factor of Mind.

Conscious Mind: Mind level aware of stimuli, inner feelings and thoughts.

Core Beliefs: Fundamental belief about self, whether true or not.

Count Down: Induction method counting down while offering relaxation suggestions between numbers.

Counselor: A mental health professional specializing in adjustment problems not mental disorders.

Counter Suggestion: Suggestion given to a person to displace or challenge a core or fixed belief..

Convincers: Challenges performed in hypnosis to prove hypnotic state has occurred.

Covert: An adjective applied to internal activities of organisms that ordinarily can be observed only with the aid of special instruments.

Critical Factor: A theoretical concept explaining the separation of conscious and subconscious as a filter that filters conscious messages to the subconscious. This is by-passed in hypnosis.

Cueing: A valuable technique used to increase client compliance with medical treatment. Linking hypnotic suggestion in the client's mind to the act of, for example, taking medication.

D

Davis & Husband Scale: An alternate way of determining different hypnotic stage depths. Hypnotic scale showing 30 effects that can be achieved at various depth of hypnosis. Effects are place into four general categorical states.

Debriefing: A ratification of trance experience upon emerging from state.

Deepening (Intensifying) Techniques: Traditionally used to intensify client hypnotic state after formal induction has been administered (stairs, elevator, compounding, silence, etc.)

Defense Mechanism: A system of self-protection devices designed to lessen or repress certain thoughts, memories, or feelings from entering the conscious mind.

Delusion: A false belief /idea. An irrational belief tenaciously held in spite of all evidence to the contrary.

Delta Rhythms: 4 HRZ; Rather slow rhythms in the EEG, characteristic of light sleep.

Delta State: Deepest state of brain activity. An extreme state of suggestibility sometimes referred to as the comatose / dreamless state.

Dendrite: A tree-like extension of the neuron cell body; receives information from other neurons.

Detachment: When client is aware of his environment, but doesn't care to participate in it.

Depersonalization: A temporary loss of self-identity or of subjective based reality.

Direct Suggestion: Non-Permissive, Paternal or commanding direction.

Disengagement (De-hypnotization): Final state of hypnotic interaction that ends the trance state.

Displacement: A hypnotic technique used in pain management, displaces pain to another area of the body, or outside of the body.

Dissociated: Viewing/experiencing an event from outside one's own body. Example: Seeing yourself on a movie screen. Floating above an event and seeing yourself. Contrast with Associated.

Dissociation: A way to distance or separate a person by suggestion from a scene or event where it may be uncomfortable or painful. Normally the recalling of memories is a result of the association of ideas. If there is a failure in the ability to recall events, which normally should be remembered, it is termed "dissociation" -- an interruption of the memory.

The concept of dissociation is widely used, but poorly defined. By "dissociation of awareness" we mean a separation or segregation off from awareness of a group of mental processes. In the induction of hypnosis there is apparently a stage during which consciousness is highly constricted, that is dissociated from that which would normally constitute its content.

Dissociation of Awareness: A selective constriction of awareness, which excludes all sources of stimulation, except for the suggestions of the hypnotist.

Dissociative Language: A hallmark of trance state and also a deepener and convincer of trance. The MORE that hand feels separated from the body, the MORE hypnotic experience is ratified.

Distortion: The condition in which certain elements of our personality, as they relate to the external world, become crystallized into certain rigid/outdated modes of perceptions.

Double Blind Suggestion: Suggestion of choice where either choice is the same: Darned if you do, darned if you don't.

Double Negative: A hypnotic language pattern, allowing some clients to accept the suggestion more than a positive suggestion. EX: You cannot (or TRY NOT) to pay attention to the warmth developing in the soles of your feet." In this case, two negatives negate each other to form a positive suggestion; (a hint of confusion enhances acceptance, as well.)

Duration: A measured or estimated period of time while in hypnotic state.

E

Ecology: From the biological sciences; concern for the whole person/organization as a balanced, interacting system. When a change is ecological, the whole person and organization (or family) benefits.

EEG (Electroencephalograph): Device detecting & graphically displaying micro currents of brainwave activity.

Effectors: The organs (muscles or glands) that perform the actual response functions of adjustment.

Efferent Neurons: Neuron that carries messages from the CNS to an organ of response. Also known as motor neuron.

Eidetic Imagery: Sensory imagery, primarily visual, which practically reaches the clarity of actual perception.

Embedded Suggestion: Bypassing the conscious mind, hypnotist encourages an inward focus embedded in the words: "Going deep INside can be very INteresting... IN there, where you employ your ImagINation, fascINation, INtuition.

Emerge: To bring out of trance state.

Emotion: Internal or visceral activity. The body is designed to understand emotional chemicals.

Emotional Behavior: Behavior that is activated by the ANS.

Emotional Outlet: A learned action or way to release emotional energy.

Empathy: The ability to perceive and attune to the feelings, energies and emotional states of another person without becoming identified with them. An intellectual identification with or vicarious experiencing of the feelings, thoughts or attitudes of another. Empathy connects us to client.

Empowerment: The process of giving power and authority to another person so he or she can feel challenged and involved and ultimately satisfied with his or her accomplishments.

Endorphins: Any of several peptides secreted in the brain that have a pain-relieving effect like that of morphine. These analgesic chemicals are naturally produced by the body. Neurotransmitters produced in the brain that generate cellular and behavioral effects like those of morphine.

Engagement: A safe reference to the term Hypnotic Trance State.

Epinephrine: A hormone, released by the adrenal medulla and the brain that acts with nor epinephrine to activate the sympathetic division of the autonomic nervous system. Sometimes called adrenaline.

EPC (Etheric Plane Communication): A way of communicating to another person through the use of active imagination and also to communicate with different parts of oneself.

Evoked Potentials: A measure of the brain's electrical activity in response to sensory stimuli. This is obtained by placing electrodes on the surface of the scalp (or more rarely, inside the head), repeatedly administering a stimulus, and then using a computer to average the results.

Euphoria: real or suggested conditions of extreme well being or pleasure.

Excitation: A change in the electrical state of a neuron that is associated with an enhanced probability of action potentials.

Expectancy: Creation of outcome for the client; how life will be different once goal is attained.

Extrovert: A person whose interest is directed toward the thoughts, feelings and ideals present in the external world; often perceived as outgoing and gregarious.

Eye-Accessing Cues: Unconscious movements of the eyes that let us know if someone is seeing images, hearing sounds or experiencing feelings.

F

Facilitator: In Hetero Hypnosis, the guide or operator of the client's experience.

Fascination Point: The object/place that a person focuses their attention on when using an eyes open hypnotic method.

First Position: Viewing/experiencing the world through one's own eyes and with one's own body. See Associated.

Fixation: Focused concentration of attention on a single sensation or object.

Fluff: This refers to meaningless filler included in induction, or in the story. It is meaningless detail thought to bore the client and deepen trance awareness and absorption of message. Just a few well-placed suggestions inserted amidst a flurry of fluff may become more effective than a didactic (purposeful) suggestion.

Forensic Hypnosis: Legal application of hypnosis.

Forebrain: The largest division of the brain, which includes the cerebral cortex and basal ganglia. It is credited with the highest intellectual functions.

Fractionation: A series of inductions, bringing a subject up out of trance and then leading them back down for the purpose of increasing their hypnotic depth.

Free Association: The association or connection of ideas/feelings that are formed in the absence of any external interference. The spontaneous outpouring of subconscious material without the thought of editing or censoring it.

Free Floating Anxiety: Feelings of dread or apprehension that cannot be traced to a particular source.

Frontal lobes: Located behind the forehead. Closely linked with making decisions and judgments.

Functional Disorders: Disorders that are of a somatic nature with the cause being of a mental origin or influence – e.g., hysterical paralysis, blindness or deafness.

Future Pace / Future Pacing: A process for connecting resource states to specific cues in one's future so that resources will automatically reoccur; create time distortion. Also see *Anchor, Resource State*.

G

Galvanic Skin Response (GSR): Increase in voltage and/or change in electrical resistance of the skin occurring during emotion as a result of action of the ANS on the sweat glands.

Gamma-Amino Butyric Acid (GABA): An amino acid transmitter in the brain whose primary function is to inhibit the firing of neurons.

Gastrointestinal Tract: The digestive tract, from mouth to anus.

Gestalt Therapy: A psychotherapy developed by Fritz Perls and others that emphasizes immediate experience and participation of the whole person in any activity.

Glia: Specialized cells that nourish and support neurons.

Glove Anesthesia: The technique whereby a person is taught to anesthetize their hand and then transfer that numbed condition to other parts of their body for pain control.

Glutamate: An amino acid neurotransmitter that acts to excite neurons. Glutamate probably stimulates N-methyl-D-aspartate (NMDA) receptors that have been implicated in activities ranging from learning and memory to development and specification of nerve contacts in a developing animal. Stimulation of NMDA receptors may promote beneficial changes; while over stimulation may be the cause of nerve cell damage or death in neurological trauma and stroke.

Goal: The object of a motivated and directed sequence of behavior.

H

Habit Formation: A learned process of reacting, partly conscious and partly unconscious, brought about through repetition of a certain action of some sort.

Hallucination: Sensory experience arising apart from corresponding external stimulation. Usually an indication of a psychosis, delirium or drug addiction. Sensory impression of external objects in the absence of external stimulus.

Head Nod: Convincer; proving client is following directions / Deepening Technique

Hebbian Learning: Theory of persistence or repetition of a reverbratory activity tends to induce lasting cellular changes that add to its stability: cells that fire together, wire together.

Hetroaction: A progressively increasing tendency of an individual to respond to other suggestions after being made to respond to a number of previous suggestions; a generalization of suggestibility.

Heterohypnosis: The use of words or verbal hypnosis provided by hypnotist for client.

Hippocampus: This area plays a crucial role in processing information involving long-term memory. Damage to the hippocampus will produce global retrograde amnesia, or the inability to store information.

Homoaction: The tendency of an ideomotor response to increase in strength if it is elicited a number of times within a certain interval of time; accumulates with multiple repetitions of a suggestion.

Homeostasis: The tendency of organisms to maintain internal equilibrium.

Hormones: Chemical messengers secreted by endocrine glands to regulate the activity of target cells. They play a role in sexual development, calcium and bone metabolism, growth and many other activities.

Hyperaesthesia: An exaggerated heightening of the senses, especially tactile stimuli; can sometimes be achieved under hypnosis.

Hyperhydrosis: Excessive perspiration, usually from the hands, feet and armpits sometimes experienced during Hypnosis.

Hypermnesia: Memory recall improves with retrieval of forgotten information. The brain stores everything, forgets nothing, and most memories can be recovered when the proper association pathways are stimulated. In regression, client experiences what they REMEMBER.

Hypersuggestibility: The capacity to respond to suggestions above a norm. The subject who is readily influenced and achieves a profound level of hypnosis is said to be hypersuggestible.

Hypnagogic: The intermediate state between wakefulness and sleep; Theta brain waves.

Hypnogogic Images: Unusually vivid mental imagery associated with hypnosis. The period immediately preceding sleep and other unusual states of consciousness; the intermediate state between wakefulness and sleep.

Hypnoamnesia: Providing client suggestion so client won't remember suggestion

Hypnoanalysis: The use of hypnosis in combination with psychoanalytic techniques to get to the root of the problem. Psychoanalysis performed under hypnosis by licensed health care workers.

Hypnodisc: A spiral spinning disc used to induce trance.

Hypnodontics: The science of using hypnosis in the field of dentistry.

Hypnology: The study of sleep or brain state of hypnosis. Hypnosis is not sleep.

Hypnonarcosis: The hypnotic state brought about through the use of certain drugs i.e., Sodium Pentothal.

Hypnopompic State: Half aware, half asleep, similar to lucid dreaming.

Hypnos: The Greek god of sleep; also the origin of the word hypnosis coined by James Braid.

Hypnosis: A natural state of the nervous system that is characterized by increased suggestibility. An altered, shifting state of consciousness that can be purposefully induced to access subconscious material, heighten suggestibility, and focus attention. Safety is expanded and focus is narrowed to select elements. *Webster's: A repressed state of mental functioning in which ideas are accepted by suggestion rather than logical evaluation. Suggestions during focused attention to create change.*

Hypnotherapy: Using hypnosis is the context of therapy; use of psychotherapeutic techniques.

Hypnoidal: A very light state of hypnosis; the state in which the first effects of hypnosis are felt.

Hypnotic Languaging: Imagine, wonder, discover, curious, explore and interesting activate feelings of wonderment, which might enhance trance process.
Hypnotic: Pertaining to or associated with hypnotism.
Hypnotic State: The by-pass of subconscious critical factor to establish selective acceptable thinking.
Hypnotic Regression: Process, by which a subject vividly relives, under hypnosis, experiences which he has forgotten or repressed.
Hypnotism: The science of hypnosis; the study and use of suggestion management.
Hypnotist: The person conducting or aiding in the well-being of a client by means of hypnosis.
Hypnotizability: Refers to suggestibility or individual susceptibility to hypnosis.
Hypnotic Susceptibility: A personality characteristic that determines a subject's ability to be hypnotized and to attain a given depth of hypnosis.
Hypothalamus: A small area at the base of the brain that regulates many aspects of motivation and emotion, particularly hunger, thirst, and sexual behavior.
Hysteria: An emotional state of excitability due to mental causes.

I

Identification: A process in personality development in which a person becomes like an admired person by incorporating their goals and values into his or her own behavior.
Ideomotor Response: Involuntary movement of the body by the subconscious as a result of a suggestion or question. A muscular or motor response to an idea held in the mind either *yes or no*.
Ideosensory Action: The involuntary capacity of the brain to evoke sensory images; these may be kinesthetic, auditory, visual, olfactory, gustatory or tactile.
Idiopathic: A medical doctor has ruled out all other known cases for malaise.
Illusion: A common misperception of some sensory stimulus. All sensory modalities are subject to illusions. Image Ideal: Creation notion of: What would happen if the client became what they wanted to be.
Imagery: The ability to perceive or mentally recreate ideas, picture or feelings; includes responses in all sensory classifications. Imagery is not all visual. It is possible to imagine, in varying degrees, other kinds of sensory impressions (sounds, odor, taste, touch, etc.).
Imagination: The ability of the mind to construct and reorganize sensory data from an experience of our outer or inner world- either real or imagined; the bridge between body and mind.

Immediate Memory: A phase of memory that is extremely short-lived, with information stored only for a few seconds. It also is known as short-term and working memory.

Implication: Indirect method of suggestion that stimulates trance by conveying positive expectancy: WHEN you are aware of warmth starting to spread out, you may nod your head....WHICH one of your hands is lighter: implying one is lighter; Take all the time you need and WHEN your subconscious is ready, your yes finger can move all by itself: (Ideomotor Response).

Imprint: Strong emotion attached to past experience created by external and internal stimulus.

Imprinting: A rapid and relatively permanent type of learning that occurs within a limited period of time, usually early in life.

Incongruence: When goals, thoughts and behaviors are in conflict.

Indirect Hypnosis: The production of hypnosis without the subject's awareness.

Induction: The act of inducing, causing, preparing or producing the state of hypnosis.

Inhibition: In reference to neurons, it is a synaptic message that prevents the recipient cell from firing.

Inner Child: An archetypal image representing our emotional/feeling center or body.

Insight: A sudden reorganization of the elements of a problem causing the solution to become self-evident. Also, one's understanding of one's own behavior or motives.

Insomnia: The inability to sleep caused by emotional or mental reasons.

Instinct: Inborn behavior or response of a species.

Intention: The desire or goal of a behavior. Intention is presumed to be positive.

Interactive Hypnosis: Hypnotherapy where the therapist and client interact verbally, the client takes a more active role in the healing process.

Interspersal: The hypnotist's patter (language patterns) that is frequently interspersed with repeated key words, phrases, metaphors or anecdotes to indirectly influence client. Narrating between countdown numbers, set apart by pause, potentiates the suggestion.

Interview: The time when a therapist gathers information and establishes rapport with a client.

Introspection: A psychological technique used to examine one's own conscious experience; self-observation of one's thoughts, feelings, and emotions.

Introvert: A person whose interest is directed inward to one's own thoughts, feelings and ideals; often perceived as quiet and reserved.

I.S.E.: Initial Sensitizing Event.

K

Keyword: A word or collection of words repeated frequently during hypnotic state to be used as post-hypnotic dialog.

Kinesis: Body Movement

Kinesthetic: Muscles, tendons and organs stimulated by body movement. Also refers to learning input through emotions as well. Sensory modality of touch, muscle tension (sensations) and emotions (feelings.)

Kinesthesis: Muscle, tendon and joint sensitivities.

L

Lachrymation: Tearing of the eyes while in hypnotic state; physical sign of trance (ratification).

Law of Dominant Effect: That perception which has the greatest emotive power tends to be the one that most influences the system.

Law of Parsimony: Law states that hypnotist should say or do as little as is necessary to achieve the desired response; less-is-more approach: Sit back now, close your eyes, and let yourself go into trance.

Law of Reciprocity: Give people more than they expect to receive.

Law of Reverse Action: A suggestion that reverses itself in the subconscious mind; *the harder you try to do something, the more difficult it is to do.*

Leading: NLP Technique designed to gently guide the client into suggestion management.

Left Cerebral Hemisphere: This part of the brain is most closely associated with consciousness. The left hemisphere usually manages the right side of the body, controls language and general cognitive functions. It plays a predominate role in deciding what responses are made to incoming stimuli.

Lethargic State: An extremely relaxed state in which the subject may display symptoms of slurred speech, inability to move. Through suggestion a subject can override natural reflex reactions to sensory stimulation.

Limbic System: A collection of interconnected brain structures whose functions include smell and emotional reactions and conditioning. Contains a number of interconnected brain structures which are linked to hormones, drives, temperature control, emotion, and, to memory formation. Neurons affecting heart rate and respiration are concentrated in the hypothalamus and direct most of the physiological changes that accompany strong emotion.

Long-Term Memory: Final phase of memory in which information storage lasts from hours to a lifetime.

M

Mania: A mental disorder characterized by excessive excitement. A form of psychosis with exalted feelings, delusions of grandeur, elevated mood, psychomotor over activity and overproduction of ideas.

Manic: Extremely excited, hyperactive or irritable.

Matching: Developed by the late Milton Erickson, and used by John Grinder and Richard Bandler in their system of neurolinguistic programming (NLP). The technique consists of adopting parts of another person's behavior, such as particular gestures, facial expressions, forms of speech, tone of voice and so on. Done skillfully, it helps create rapport.

Memory Consolidation: The physical and psychological changes that take place as the brain organizes and restructures information in order to make it a permanent part of memory.

Mental Rehearsal: A way of using the imagination to rehearse what a certain condition or action will be like at some point in the future.

Merging: The process whereby a person allows a greater flow of psychic/emotional energy into their body/mindarising from contact with one's own archetypes. (Hand Merge)

Mesmerism: The name given to those practices of Anton Mesmer as related to animal magnetism.

Mesmerize: An archaic term for hypnotize.

Metaphor: A way of subconsciously equating or tying together two or more separate, yet related images through the use of a story. A therapeutic story that helps replace one thought with another.

Meta-Program: A mental program that operates across many different contexts of a person's life.

Mind: "Seat" of Consciousness that thinks, perceives, feels and wills.

Mindfulness: The behavior of living in the present moment.

Mirroring: Putting oneself in the same posture as another person, in order to gain rapport.

Model: A description of the essential distinctions of an experience or ability.

Modeling: (Used in NLP) A type of imitation in which an individual mimics behavior performed by another person. The process of studying living examples of human excellence in order to find the essential distinctions of thought and behavior one needs in order to get the same results.

Monoideism: James Braid's finding that the state of hypnosis depends on narrowing or limiting of subject's attention; the domination of the nervous system by one single idea.

Motor Neuron: A neuron that carries information from the central nervous system to the muscle.

Motivation: The Subconscious force behind manifesting certain desired behavior patterns carried out by Conscious mind..

Motivation Direction: (Meta-Program) A mental program that determines whether a person moves towards or away from experiences.

Multiple Personality: A form of emotional disturbance in which an individual maintains two or more distinct personalities usually with no conscious recognition between them.

Musings: Abstractive thoughts spoken by hypnotist to direct client thought.

Myelin: Compact fatty material that surrounds and insulates axons of some neurons.

N

Negative Hallucination: The failure to see an object when looking at it.

Negative Suggestion: Utilizing a sort of reverse-psychology approach, when used skillfully, may obtain client response by suggestion client NOT respond in the desired way: Do not think of your favorite color; I suggest you not notice that feeling in your hand; you shouldn't be thinking about your childhood sweetheart right now.

Negativism: Resistance to suggestions even to the extent of taking the opposite action.

Neuro-Linguistic Programming: (NLP) The study of the structure of subjective experience; the process of creating models of human excellence in which the usefulness, not the truthfulness, is the most important criterion for success.

Neuron: Individual nerve cell. It is specialized for the transmission of information and characterized by long fibrous projections called axons, and shorter, branch-like projections called dendrites.

Neuroplasticity: The brain's ability to compensate for lost function.

Neuro-Semantics: The science of the effect that words have on the human nervous system.

Neurosis (Neurotic): A behavior disturbance primarily characterized by excessive anxiety, minor distortions of reality, and subjective reality.

Neurotransmitter: A chemical released by neurons at a synapse for the purpose of relaying information by way of receptors.

Non-Sequitur Suggestions: Used to interrupt or distract the mind in trance, the statement is out of context and can de-potentiate conscious mental sets. A confusion technique overloading (distracting) the conscious mind. Non-sequiturs can be any phrase or question: Do you like the sound of the rain on the roof?

Non-Verbal Shifts: Part of rapport is pacing or mirroring of client behaviors outside of the consciousness. Match clients' breathing, mirrors a part of client not in their awareness. Then, shift breath, and client follows; they are responding to you unconsciously and are in a state of high suggestibility.

O

Objectivity: An attitude unaffected by personal feelings or prejudice; unbiased.

Obsessions: Recurring irrational or disturbing thoughts a person cannot prevent. A driving, irresistible idea and when combined with emotion, is likely to result in action, sometimes endlessly repeated.

Obsessive-compulsive Disorder: Extreme preoccupation with certain thoughts and/or compulsive performance of certain behaviors, both of which occur in ritualistic or unavoidable fashion.

Operator: Synonymous with hypnotist or hypnotherapist; facilitator of hetero-hypnosis.

Or: Creates new options for different choices.

Outcome: Imagined goal recognized.

Overt: An adjective applied to behavior that can be observed without the aid of special instruments.

P

Pacing: The ability to match or pace another person's state of being. Can take the form of breath, body, language, energy level, or feeling tone pacing. Resonating, vibrating, getting in synch with another person. Intentionally matching another's behavior, posture, language/predicates to build rapport.

Pain: An uncomfortable to distressing sensation perceived either somatically or mentally. Reframe to *"discomfort"*.

Panic Disorder: Persistently high levels of anxiety coupled with sudden episodes of intense, but unfocused panic.

Paradox: A statement that seems to contradict itself; yet expresses a possibility of truth.

Paradigm: An change of perspective on an occurring event without anything happening in reality

Parasympathetic Nervous System: The division of the autonomic nervous system associated with production of relaxation, bodily sensations, and conservation of energy. That portion of the ANS that controls most of the ordinary vital functions of life, such as digestion. Its action is antithetic to that of the sympathetic division in most cases.

Parietal Lobe: One of the four subdivisions of the cerebral cortex. It plays a role in sensory processes, attention and language.

Patter: Language patterns created as a body of the hypnotic script.

Perception: The interpretation of sensation. Process of becoming aware of objects, events, and qualities that stimulate the sense organs and of determining the relationship between them.

Peripheral Nervous System: All portions of the nervous system lying outside the brain and spinal cord, including the autonomic nervous system. A division of the nervous system consisting of all nerves not part of the brain or spinal cord.

Permissive: This approach to hypnotic induction is the opposite of authoritarian. A permissive suggestion is made in such a manner as to give the subject the option of responding. The subject, no the hypnotist, is made the perceived source of the response. Permissive suggestions never have an intonation of authority or command.

Persona: In Jung's system, an archetype representing the "mask" or public self presented to others.

Personality: An individual's unique and enduring traits and psychological characteristics and the dynamic relationship among them.

Personality Disorder: Disturbances involving maladaptive and long-standing distortions of personality characteristics.

Phobia: An intense or unrealistic fear of some specific object or situation.

Physical Cues: The signs the body displays when in the hypnotic state.

Physiology of Hypnosis: According to medical authorities, all of the associated conditions that occur in hypnosis are basically identical with that of the waking rather than the sleeping state.

Placebo: A sham drug having no physiological effect, used in research to avoid the factor of suggestion.

Placebo Effect: Changes in behavior due to one's expectations that a drug or action will have some beneficial effect on them.

Positive Hallucination: Any perceptions that have no external cause or stimulus.

Positive Expectancy: Client is likely to respond when hypnotist conveys confidence and certainty that improvement can be expected. Creating positive expectancy ahead of trance induction assists client's positive change.

Positive Suggestion: The most common, useful and simple type of suggestion structure; supportive and encouraging phrases giving client the idea that s(he) can experience or accomplish something desirable: You are feeling more comfortable with every breath you inhale; you can remember a time where you felt proud of yourself; you are discovering inner strengths you didn't realize you had before.

Post Traumatic Stress Response (PTSR): Psychological and emotional disturbance following exposure to stresses outside the range of normal human experience, such as natural disasters or wars. This is a Hypnotic term rather than post traumatic stress DISORDER which is a psychological term..

Post Hypnotic Response: Acts carried out after the termination of hypnosis in response to specific suggestions are called posthypnotic. A suggestion given during hypnosis serves as the stimulus and the act becomes the response.

Post Hypnotic Suggestion: A suggestion given in the hypnotic state that is to be carried out after returning to normal, active awareness. Suggestion that becomes or remains active after the hypnotic session is over.

Potential: A possibility of that which is not yet fully realized.

Prejudice: Unreasonable feelings, opinions or attitudes, especially of a hostile nature, directed against a racial, religious or national group.

Presupposition: Assumes client response will happen; it's just a matter of when: You are pleasantly surprised when you discover these suggestions working well for you.

Prestige Suggestion: Suggestions provided by those in perceived authority: celebrities, doctors, hypnotists.

Prinz Comfort Assessment Scale: A model reframe process of pain awareness to induce comfort rather than pain.

Process-Oriented-Exercise: An exercise which gives one an opportunity to role play a conversation, practice a skill, experience a feeling or investigate a new behavior.

Process Suggestion: Sparse on detail, it leaves client free to attend to whatever details s(he) has associated to the suggested experience: You can have a memory from childhood, one that you haven't thought about in a long time; You might notice a certain pleasant sensation in your body as you sit there, breathing comfortably.

Progression: A process of progressing the client into an imagined future for the purpose of modeling.

Progressive Muscle Relaxation: Technique to induce trance; interspersed throughout hypnotic process.

Projection: Attributing one's own feelings, or unacceptable impulses onto another person as a means of defending against anxiety. The act of ascribing one's own attitudes or thoughts to someone or something else.

Pseudo-memories: False or dubious memories that a person believes to be true or accurate.

Psi Events: Paranormal events falling outside the traditional bounds of psychology and science. Includes clairvoyance, telepathy, precognition, psycho kinesis, astral projection, out of body experiences, et al.

Psychoactive Drugs: Any of a large number of substances capable of altering sensation, perception, cognition, memory, or other psychological events.

Psychoanalysis: A Freudian approach for evaluating subconscious patterns, conditions and behavior through free association, dream interpretation and transference.

Psychodrama: A technique of psychotherapy in which people act out personal conflicts in the presence of other people who play supporting parts.

Psychology: The scientific study of behavior and conscious experience.

Psychosomatic: Pertaining to bodily changes stimulated or depressed through mental influence.

Psychosomatic Disorder: A physical disorder believed to be of psychogenic origin.

Psychosomatic Illness: Disorders in which actual physical damage occurs as the result of psychological stress.

Pun: Indirect play on words causing wonderment. An embedded suggestion in a pun: Your experience IN TRANCE this morning is like an ENTRANCE into another state.

Pyramiding: Strengthening of suggestions by stacking them on top of another by repetition. Same as fractionation except subject is not yet emerged; guarantees success of next difficult challenge: goes from easy test to difficult test; same as compounding suggestions.

Q

Question: A direct question will focus attention, stimulate associations and facilitate responsiveness. Use especially when resistance is present: And the tingling in your fingers matches the pulse of your heart, do you feel it yet?

R

Rapport: A client/therapist relationship that contains levels of trust, comfort & harmony. The natural process of matching and being in alignment with another; close empathetic relationship..

Realization: While in hypnosis, listener realizes s/he cannot do something (i.e.: open eyes); deepens trance and acts as a convincer.

Recall: Detailed remembering with a minimum of memory cues.

Receptor: A cell differentiated from others in terms of its increased irritability to certain stimuli.

Receptor Molecule: A specific molecule on the surface or inside of a cell with a characteristic chemical and physical structure. Many neurotransmitters and hormones exert their effects by binding to receptors on cells..m

Reciprocal Innervations: The balance of impulses leading to the relaxation of one of a pair of antagonistic muscles as the other contracts.

Reflex: A relative simple, innate response to a particular stimulus.

Reflex Arc: Simplest neural link from receptor to effectors involving the CNS; consists of a receptor, afferent neuron, sometimes a connection neuron or neurons, efferent neuron and effectors.

Reframing: Skill creating a new appreciation or understanding for client, because of information provided by Hypnotist; re-labeling or wrapping a positive connotation around problem behavior, the client suspends current belief system and sees the problem in a new light. Almost any issue the client brings you may be reframed. The session itself may be reframed as an effort to make things better.

Regression: Returning to an earlier time of certain behaviors needing resolution. The state induced by hypnosis in which a subject relives a previous period of their life.

Reinforcing: Encourages attitudes, beliefs and behaviors with supporting repetitive ideas.

Relaxation: The somatic or psychological response factor that is brought about through the use of suggestion. One can be in hypnosis without being relaxed, however, the relaxation of mind and body is a characteristic most people associate with hypnosis. Used as an easy going approach rather than a demanding, one, it allows client to experience hypnosis without having to "perform."

Relaxation Response: Coined by Dr. Herbert Benson explaining the body's healing potential when relaxed; state of freedom from mental and physical tension.

REM (Rapid Eye Movement): Movement of the eyes occurring during times of dreaming or when accessing data in the hypnotic state.

Re-parenting: The process of bringing underdeveloped parts of the psyche into contact with parts that are more mature and conscious; Transpersonal hypnotism.

Repetition: Reinforcing basic important suggestions by repeating suggestion 2—20 times.

Repression: Pushing out or barring from consciousness unwanted memories, feelings, or impulses.

Resistance: Unwillingness to be hypnotized by the subject. May be due to anxiety, misinformation, past failures, negativity or feared loss of control. To reduce resistance, cover suggestions with all possibilities - knowing/not knowing, metaphors, stories, confusion techniques, asking client question which must be answered NO.

Resource State: Regressing to positive memories to bolster client confidence in change.

Retrograde Amnesia: Loss of memory for events that happened before amnesia producing event.

Revivication: A reliving of a prior period (or trauma) of life. In revivification the hypnotized person returns to a physiological state believed to have existed at the time to which the client has returned. All memories following the age to which the client has been regressed are removed.

Rigidity: The condition whereby muscles become extremely tense.

Right cerebral hemisphere: Controls the left half of the body. In most people it manages nonverbal processes, such as attention, pattern recognition, line orientation; detection of complex auditory tones.

Rod: A sensory neuron located in the periphery of the retina. It is sensitive to light of low intensity and specialized for nighttime vision.

Role Reversal: Taking the role of another person to learn how one's own behavior appears from their perspective; or to understand their perspective better.

S

Safe Place / Space: Allows client to find a place of safety within them to return to while in trance.

Secondary Gain: about an illness means that the patient "needs" the illness to solve some other problem. Client is unlikely to be motivated to resolve medical problems, if that also means giving up the solution.

Second Position: Viewing/experiencing an event from the perspective of the person you are interacting with.

Seeding: A suggestion may be more successful when it has been mentioned, or seeded, beforehand. A target suggestion is seeded, and later, hypnotist mentions the suggestion again, and the target is activated. Used also as a pre-hypnotic.

Selective Attention: A psychological characteristic of the hypnotic state, client can NOT notice what they choose not to notice. The ability to deliberately focus on one portion of an experience while turning out the rest: Pay attention to the sound of my voice allowing all other sounds to become unimportant background noise.

Selective Awareness: State of mind (mental process) and alert concentration; the inability of the conscious mind to picture more than one concept at a time.

Self-Actualization: The full development of personal potential, especially emotional potential.

Self-Esteem: Persistent, unfailing belief that you are a worthy human being.

Self-Hypnosis: Hypnosis induced by oneself to influence positive self-improvement

Semantics: The science of the meaning of words. Technique for sharpening the accuracy of thinking; emphasizes the need for operational definitions of words and the importance of avoiding the tendency to regard words as things rather than as mere names for concepts

Semantic Conditioning: Refers to the formation of conditioned responses to the meanings of verbal stimuli rather than their physical attributes (i.e. the sound of a word).

Sensation: The un-interpreted experience accompanying afferent activity that reaches the cortical level.

Sensitization: A change in behavior or biological response by an organism that is produced by delivering a strong, generally noxious, stimulus.

Sensory Hyperesthesia: Hyper acute senses in trance state.

Sensory Modalities: The 5 senses through which we take in experience: sight, hearing, touch, taste, smell.

Set Point: A theoretical proportion of body fat that tends to be maintained even with alterations in hunger and eating; *a fat thermostat.*

Shaman: In various cultures the one who would heal, assist, or help others through certain conditions using techniques of known and unknown origin.

Short-Term Memory: A phase of memory in which a limited amount of information may be held for several seconds to minutes.

Silence: Also known as Pregnant Pauses, deepens trance: Take a moment to feel 10 - 100 times more relaxed before I return to your thoughts.

Simile: A way of directly and consciously comparing two different images.

Socialization: A process of learning to live in a particular environment; adopting socially acceptable behaviors.

Somatic Bridge Induction: A technique to rapidly access a person's subconscious material.

Somatic Therapy: Any therapy directly involving bodily processes.

Somatoform: A class of disturbances characterized by exaggerated bodily complaints (hypochondria) or by the presence of physical disability without apparent cause.

Somnambulism: In everyday usage the term somnambulism is used for sleepwalking, however in the lexicon of hypnotism, somnambulism is used to designate the deepest state of hypnosis. Eyes may be open without waking; complete amnesia may result; the deepest state of hypnosis.

Speaking the client's language: Literally using the client's own words allows suggestions to conform more to the client's thinking and be more effective.

Spontaneous Remission: Spontaneous disappearance of psychological symptoms or behavioral disturbances.

Stimulus: A change brought about in a receptor by a signal from the environment. Any physical energy that has some effect on an organism and that evokes a response.

Strategy: A sequence of internal representations and behavior leading to an outcome.

Stress: A reaction or response coming from the nervous system to what is being perceived as a threat; unmanaged stress is thought to be at the root cause of most physical and psychological disease.

Stroop effect: A pause in the delivery of hypnotic suggestion to create deepening of hypnotic subject; A demonstration of the reaction time of a task.

Subconscious Mind: The psychic processes of which an individual is not conscious. They are often associated with the part of the mind involving imagination, memory and creativity. The subconscious mind is particularly accessible through hypnotic suggestion.

Subject: This term denotes an individual submitting to an induction of hypnosis. If hypnosis is being used for hypnotherapy, the term *client* is a better word to use.

Subjective Time: Time as perceived by a subject (as opposed to real time).

Subliminal: Perception of a stimulus that is presented below the threshold of conscious recognition.

Submodalities: The components that make up a Sensory Modality. Example: In the visual Modality, the submodalities include color, brightness, focus dimensionality, etc.

Subpersonalities: Secondary personalities that are formed as a means of self-protection from trauma, neglect, pain, etc. Coping mechanisms for our psyche.

Suggestibility: The capacity to respond to suggestion. The propensity of a subject to accept and act on suggestion.

Suggestibility Test: A series of actions performed by a person to show the hypnotherapist, as well as the client, the degree and type of suggestibility one has.

Suggestion: A word, words and/or gestures used to create or convey an idea or image. Hypnotic communication. An idea conveyed to the mind by an action or through the spoken word.

Synchronicity: Coincidence of events that seem to be meaningfully related; stems from Jungian theory as an explanatory principle on the same order as causality.

Synthesia: Combines elements of thought into a whole idea.

Syntony: An occurrence that one becomes aware of a split second before it happens.

Symbol: An image, object or activity that represents and can be substituted for something else. For example, words and numbers.

Sympathetic Nervous System (SNS): Division of the ANS (autonomic nervous system) that is active in emergency conditions of extreme cold, violence, exercise and states of fear or rage. Responsible in times of emotion or stress for activating the body by speeding up energy consumption and preparing the body for action.

Synapse: A gap between two neurons that functions as the site of information transfer from one neuron to another.

T

Tasking: Before Hypnotization, agreement with client to become responsible for their own outcome.

Temporal Lobe: One of the four major subdivisions of each hemisphere of the cerebral cortex. It functions in auditory perception, speech and complex visual perceptions.

Thalamus: A structure consisting of two egg-shaped masses of nerve tissue, each about the size of a walnut, deep within the brain. It is the key relay station for sensory information flowing into the brain, filtering out only information of particular importance from mass of signals entering the brain.

Therapy: Remedial service or curative process for medical or mental disorder.

Theta State: Deeply relaxed state, often called the threshold to sleep and sometimes called the somnambulistic state. In this condition a person may display slurred speech, rigidity of limbs, and amnesia of the experience upon awakening.

Third Position: Viewing/experiencing an event as an observer from the outside.

Time Distortion: A condition in which time seems to have either sped up or slowed down. This subjective experience seems longer or shorter than in reality; often observed in the hypnotic state.

Timeline: The unconscious arrangement of a person's past memories and future expectations. Typically, this is a "line" of images.

Trance: Mental concentration; a term widely used by Milton Erickson and his followers. The term trance is often used synonymously for hypnosis. A particular state of the nervous system obtained in hypnosis. By extension, every hypnotic state: light trance, medium trance, deep trance, etc.

Trance Logic: The suspension of critical judgment on the part of a hypnotized subject and his or her ability to tolerate the coexistence of logically incompatible phenomena.

Transratification: After the hypnotic experience, proving to the client that they were hypnotized; i.e. Time distortion.

Transference: Refers to the tendency of a person to transfer various feelings to the therapist that corresponds to feelings held toward other persons in their life.

Truism: A commonsense observation appearing so self-evident as to be virtually an undeniable statement of fact: Everyone has felt a warmth of the sun on their skin. Series of truisms leads to Yes-Sets building a commitment and acceptance of ideas.

U

Unconditioned Reflex (Response) (UR): A response that occurs to appropriate stimulation without prior conditioning.

Unconditioned Stimulus (US): A stimulus that affects behavior without prior learning.

Unconscious: A lack of consciousness / unaware of all senses.

Unconscious Mind: A term used in psychiatry to denote a postulated region of the psyche, the repository of repressed urges and wishes; collective unconscious is also referred to the Unconscious Mind.

Utilization: An induction technique using the surroundings (temperature, yawn, feeling of body) and it is also a therapy that tailors into account the client's unique motivations, interest, preferences and use of language.

V

Visual: Sensory modality of seeing.

W

Waking Hypnosis: While in the waking state a person is actually under the influence of a post-hypnotic suggestion.

Wernicke's Area: A region of the brain responsible for the comprehension of language and the production of meaningful speech.

Y

Yes-Set: Involves mentioning truisms, or aspects of undeniable reality allowing client to be more receptive to suggestion.

www.ingramcontent.com/pod-product-compliance
Lightning Source LLC
Chambersburg PA
CBHW080732230426
43665CB00020B/2714